Contents

Part 1: Studying the evidence — 2
1 Guidelines and fakes — 2
2 Receptive minds — 4

Part 2: Towards war: 1937–9 — 6
3 Hitler and Europe 1937 — 6
4 Vienna 1938 — 8
5 Munich 1938 — 10
6 A Jew in Berlin — 12
7 Summer 1939 — 14
8 Hitler Youth 1939 — 16

Part 3: Britain alone — 18
9 The 'Phoney War', 1939–40 — 18
10 Blackout, barrage balloons and the Home Guard — 20
11 Blitzkrieg 1940 — 22
12 Dunkirk — 24
13 Battle of Britain — 26
14 'Blitz' — 28

Part 4: Worldwide war 1941 — 30
15 War at sea — 30
16 Lease-lend — 32
17 Hitler's plans and Fortress Europe — 34
18 Barbarossa — 36
19 Desert war — 38
20 The Far East — 40
21 Japan strikes: Pearl Harbour — 42

22 — 44
23 — 44
24 — 46
24 El Alamein — 48
25 At Monte Cassino 1943 — 50
26 Pacific War 1 — 52
27 Pacific War 2 — 54
28 Germany bombed — 56
29 The Allies work together — 58

Part 6: Partisans, prisoners and war production — 60
30 Partisans 1 — 60
31 Partisans 2 — 62
32 Prisoners — 64
33 The final solution — 66
34 British women at war — 68
35 Scientists go to war — 70

Part 7: The ring closes 1944–5 — 72
36 D-Day — 72
37 Advance into Germany — 74
38 Germany in despair — 76
39 Berlin: death and glory — 78
40 Kamikaze — 80
41 The atomic bomb — 82

Part 8: Costs and consequences — 84
42 The cost of victory — 84
43 Home fronts 1945 — 86
44 Potsdam and a divided Germany — 88
45 Nuremburg — 90
46 Refugees and repatriation — 92
47 Writers and the war — 94
Further reading — 96

Part 1

Studying the evidence

1 Guidelines and fakes

All the extracts, pictures and maps in this book relate to a confused and complicated period of world-wide war. During any war each side often falsifies events or stops the publication of information either to mislead the enemy or build up morale at home.

You should ask three questions in relation to any extract from a piece of writing or any picture:

1 Who wrote the piece or produced the picture?
2 When exactly was it produced and what other events were going on at the time?
3 Why was it produced and who was intended to see or read it?

For a photograph you should consider carefully whether or not it was posed and, if it was, does it give a realistic idea of the actual atmosphere? When you consider accounts of an event, remember that people often see or hear what they expect to see or hear. Writers sometimes say that they were present at an event when, in fact, they were on the edge of the main action. People who were close enough to be eyewitnesses were often distracted because so many things happened at once. Modern battles are difficult to understand for these reasons. Above all, take note of how soon after an event any account was written. Memory can be very selective. When you read extracts from a novel or poem remember that they do not try to describe exactly how events happened but to give an idea of what it felt like to be there.

A   A deliberate fake

In May 1944 cheering crowds greeted General Sir Bernard Montgomery in Gibraltar. In fact Montgomery (left) was in England and his place in Gibraltar had been taken by Clifton James (right), an actor. These pictures show how well Montgomery's double deceived the crowds.

B An artistic fake

In February 1945 the Americans lost 6000 soldiers in the fight to capture the island of Iwo Jima from the Japanese. The picture of the raising of the American flag on Mount Suribachi became a frozen moment symbolising this struggle to the world. In fact two flags were raised and the official photograph (left) showed the planting of the first flag by the Marines. A more famous photograph was taken by Joe Rosenthal, a photographer who had landed three hours after the first invasion, just as the second flag was being put up. Rosenthal took a snap (right) of the US marines before they posed for the official photograph, and it was this shot, not the posed picture, or the original flag raising, that became famous throughout the world.

Questions

1 Who was intended to see the photograph on the right in Source A? What were they meant to believe?

2 How does its date help you to work out the reasons for the fake?

3 Look at Source B. Why do you think the marines replaced the small flag with a larger flag?

4 Which of the two flag-raising pictures is an action picture and which posed?

5 If you were the picture editor of a newspaper which of the pictures would you print?

6 Some people say that Rosenthal's photograph was posed and faked because the first small flag was the real flag raising. Discuss this argument.

2 Receptive minds

Deception only works if people are prepared to believe what they read. This sometimes works because they are anxious for news of any sort like Squash, the soldier in Source A. The extract is taken from a book The Fortress *which was published in 1958 and written by Richard Trevelyan, who was an officer in the Rifle Brigade and fought against the Germans in Italy. He describes how he found Squash sending home propaganda leaflets scattered by the Germans (or 'Tedeschi', as British troops in Italy called them).*

A German propaganda

The other type of leaflet is anti-American. For instance, a woman in a petticoat is shown sitting on a crumpled bed as she pulls on a stocking, whilst a G.I. straightens his tie in front of the mirror. The caption for this is: 'What goes on at home whilst you are away? No woman can resist such handsome brutes from the wideopen spaces.' Then there is another, entitled 'You Americans are sooooo wonderful', showing two abandoned un-British-looking hausfraus hanging round a G.I.'s neck. . . .

Banal and crashingly stupid though all this propaganda is, there's no doubt that it's having an effect on the likes of Squash, who seems to have lost all his bounce recently. Gone are the tales, bawdy or otherwise. Nowadays it's nothing but grouse, grouse, grouse. Why are we here at all at Anzio? Why don't we get a move on, or clear out? What's the use of wasting men, wasting money? 'I don't want to kill a Tedeschi, any more than he wants to kill me.' Blah, blah.

The boredom does get you down, and there's no doubt that one's nerves are worn thin by the mere lack of news and the nagging feeling all the time that something is brewing up. We do nothing but watch and wait.

From R. Trevelyan, *The Fortress*, Collins, 1958.

B Invasion preparations

In 1944 the Germans expected the main Allied landing to be in the Calais area. This belief was strengthened by a number of Allied tricks. One of these was to create dummy concentrations of troops and tanks in South-East England. The picture shows a dummy tank, which was blown up in the same way as a barrage balloon.

Questions

1 What did the German leaflet aim to make the American and British soldiers worry about?

2 What evidence is there in the passage that the propaganda had an effect? Does it suggest that the leaflets alone were responsible?

3 How far do you think that the old saying 'there is no smoke without fire' is shown to be true in this extract?

4 How good a fake do you think the tank in Source B would have been?

5 There is evidence that the Germans were not sure when or where the Allies would land in Europe. Write down the sort of ways in which false information could be given. You might read: *The Man Who Never Was* by Ewen Montagu (Corgi, 1968).

Part 2

Towards war: 1937–9

3 Hitler and Europe 1937

In 1937 the boundaries of Europe were more or less the same as they had been fixed at Versailles by the powers that had won the First World War. Germany had been split in two by the 'Polish Corridor' and her ally Austria-Hungary had been cut up into several small states including Czechoslovakia. The people of Austria were German speaking and so were most of those in the Sudetenland in Western Czechoslovakia, parts of western Poland, and in the towns in the three Baltic States (Lithuania, Latvia and Estonia). The Versailles Treaty had forbidden the Anschluss (union) of Germany and Austria.

To protect these arrangements France had made treaties with Poland and Czechoslovakia, and Britain had agreed, in the Locarno Pact, to aid France if she was attacked by Germany. In Source B you can read about Hitler's view of the situation as he gave it to a secret meeting of German military leaders. His plans came as a shock to many of them. The minutes of the meeting were written by Hitler's adjutant, Colonel Hossbach.

A Europe in 1937

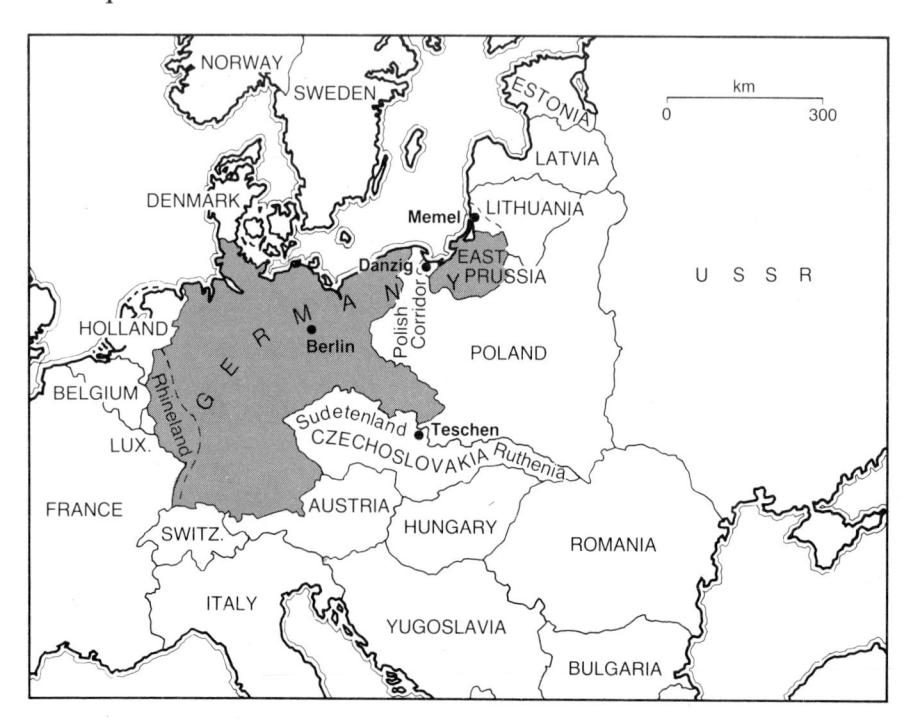

B The Hossbach memorandum

The Fuehrer then stated: The aim of German policy is the security and the preservation of the Volk and its propagation. This is consequently a problem of space ... The question for Germany is where the greatest possible conquest can be made at lowest cost. German politics must reckon with its two hateful enemies, England and France, to whom a strong German colossus in the centre of Europe would be intolerable. Both these states would oppose a further reinforcement of Germany, both in Europe and overseas. ...

If the Fuehrer is still living, then it will be his irrevocable decision to solve the German space problem no later than 1943–1945... For the improvement of our military political position it must be our first aim, in every case of entanglement by war, to conquer Czechoslovakia and Austria simultaneously, in order to remove any threat from the flanks in case of a possible advance westward ... Once Czechoslovakia is conquered – and a mutual frontier of Germany-Hungary is obtained. ...

The Fuehrer believes personally, that in all probability England and perhaps also France, have already silently written off Czechoslovakia .... Without England's support it would also not be necessary to take into consideration a march by France through Holland and Belgium. Naturally, we should in every case have to secure our frontier during the operation of our attacks against Czechoslovakia and Austria ....

Military preparation by Russia must be countered by the speed of our operations; it is a question whether this needs to be taken into consideration at all, in view of Japan's attitude ...

From L. L. Snyder, Fifty Major Documents of the Twentieth Century, Anvil Books, Van Nostrand, 1955.

Questions

1. Use the map to explain why the 'Polish Corridor' and the free city of Danzig divided Germany into two.

2. Suggest reasons why Italy would be concerned about Hitler's plans for Austria and Czechoslovakia.

3. In which countries might Hitler expect to find some support for his plans to give Germans more living space?

4. What did Hitler mean by 'the Volk'?

5. Was there a real 'problem of space' for the Volk?

6. Use the map and the memorandum to make a step by step diagram or flow chart to explain how Hitler viewed France and England and intended to deal with them.

7. Explain the two calculations Hitler made about Russia.

8. Imagine you were present at a private meeting of two generals who had listened to Hitler's plans. One was enthusiastic and one very worried. What argument would each use to back up his attitude?

4 Vienna 1938

In February 1938 Georg Klaar took his girl-friend to a ball in Vienna. Two weeks later Hitler took over Austria and the Klaar family's world was in ruins. The Klaars were Austrian Jews. Georg Klaar escaped to Britain where he became George Clare, a soldier in the British Army. His parents perished in the concentration camp at Auschwitz.

In 1938 the Chancellor of Austria was Kurt von Schuschnigg, a patriot and a general's son. He admired what Hitler had done for Germany but was determined to keep the Germans out of Austria. Yet Hitler was putting on the pressure. He encouraged Austrian Nazis to defy the government. They attacked non-Nazis in the streets and threw petrol bombs into Jewish synagogues.

On 9 March, 1938 Schuschnigg called for a referendum: all Austrians over twenty-four were to vote for or against a free, German, independent Austria. Schuschnigg would win such a vote, and so Hitler was not going to allow it to take place. He forced the Austrian chancellor to give way. This extract describes how George Clare's family heard the news in Vienna.

A   Schuschnigg's broadcast

So we sat in Father's study grasping at straws, groping for some shreds of reassurance, searching for a power – Italy, France, Britain, or God – to come to our aid. The music stopped. It was about quarter to eight. A breathless voice, more shouting than speaking, announced 'The Chancellor' and then Schuschnigg spoke, his voice trembling with emotion:

From George Clare, *Last Waltz in Vienna*, Macmillan, 1981.

> Austrian men and women! This day has brought us face to face with a serious and decisive situation. It is my task to inform the Austrian people about the events of this day. The Government of the German Reich presented a time-limited ultimatum to the Federal President demanding that he appoint a candidate chosen by the Reich Government to the office of Chancellor and also follow its suggestions when selecting the ministers to serve in that cabinet. Should the Federal President not accept this ultimatum German troops would begin to cross our frontiers this very hour. . . .
>
> The Federal President has instructed me to inform the nation that we are giving way to brute force. Because we refuse to shed German blood even in this tragic hour, we have ordered our armed forces, should an invasion take place, to withdraw without serious resistance, and to await the decisions of the coming hours. The Federal President has asked the army's Inspector General, General of Infantry Schilhawski, to assume command over all troops. All further orders for the armed forces will be issued by him.
> So, in this hour, I bid farewell to the people of Austria with a German word, and a wish from the bottom of my heart; 'God Save Austria'.

They played the national anthem. After the last bars of Haydn's tune we all sat in utter silence for a few moments. Then before any of us had had a chance to say anything, the sounds of hundreds of men shouting at the top of their voices could be heard. Still indistinct, still distant, it sounded threatening, none the less. Those raucous voices grew louder, were coming closer.

I rushed to the window and looked out into Nussdorferstrasse. It was still quite empty. A few moments. Then the first lorry came into sight. It was packed with shouting, screaming men. A huge swastika flag fluttered over their heads. Most of them had swastika armlets on their sleeves, some wore SA caps, some even steel helmets.

Now we could hear clearly what they were shouting: 'Ein Volk, ein Reich, ein Fuehrer!' They were chanting in chorus, followed by 'Ju-da verr-rrecke! Ju-da verr-rrecke!!' (Perish Judah!!). In English this sounds softer, less threatening, but in German, coming from a thousand throats, screaming it out in the full fury of their hate, as lorry after lorry with frenzied Nazis passed below our window, it is a sound one can never forget.

Questions

1 Why would the Klaar family think it possible that Italy might come to Austria's aid?

2 What reasons does Schuschnigg give for not using the Austrian army against Germany?

3 What does 'Ein Volk, Ein Reich, Ein Fuehrer' mean? Does it tell you anything about why the Austrian Nazis welcomed the Anschluss?

4 How would you have felt listening to the Nazi chanting? What special reasons could the Klaars have for feeling it was so terrible?

5 Georg Klaar's parents stayed in Vienna. Write a letter they might have sent to friends in Britain explaining why they had decided to stay.

5 Munich 1938

On 12 September 1938 Hitler demanded that Germans in Czechoslovakia should be allowed to unite with Germany. The French had a treaty with Czechoslovakia and Britain had one with France, but the British Prime Minister, Neville Chamberlain, persuaded the French government to agree to work out an arrangement with Hitler. Neville Chamberlain flew to Germany to explain this to Hitler on 22 September, but Hitler told him there was no time for discussion. His troops would take over the German speaking parts of Czechoslovakia on 1 October. Source B shows that, in public, Hitler said it would be the end of Germany's demands for territory. Yet there could still be war if the Czechs resisted and called on France for help. The Italian dictator, Mussolini, suggested another conference in Munich on 9 September. Here, Chamberlain, Mussolini, Hitler and the French Prime Minister, Edouard Daladier, agreed to what Hitler wanted, while the Czechs waited outside. In 1938 Paul Reynaud was Finance Minister of France and he gives an account of Munich in Source C. François-Poncet was French ambassador to Germany.

A September 21: 'Still hope'

A cartoon from Punch, *21 September 1938.*

B 26 September: extract from a speech by Hitler.

I am grateful to Mr Chamberlain for all his efforts. I have assured him that the German people desires nothing else than peace and I have also told him that I cannot go back behind the limit set to our patience. I have further assured him, and I repeat it here, that when this problem is solved there is for Germany no further territorial problem in Europe. And I have further assured him that at the moment when Czechoslovakia has solved her problem, that means when the Czechs have come to terms with their other minorities, and that peaceably and not through oppression, then I have no further interest in the Czech state. And that is guaranteed to him! We want no Czechs at all!

From E. Leiser, *A Pictorial History of Nazi Germany*, Penguin, 1962.

C 29 September: Paul Reynaud's account of Munich

At half-past one in the morning the agreement was signed. M. François-Poncet wrote: 'We were bitterly aware of the cruelty of the event. Daladier shook his head, uttered, and cursed circumstances. He refused to take part in the congratulations exchanged by the other delegates. Worst, the most painful step had not yet been taken; we had now to break the news to the Czechoslovaks who were awaiting the outcome of the Conference at their hotel. Mastney, their minister in Berlin broke into tears.'

As for Hitler, he was triumphant. He had secured complete victory ... The eagerness of the Allies 'to lick the boots of the Nazis' was to exert a tremendous influence on the course of events ... The Allies themselves laboured under a complete delusion. Following his dream, Chamberlain stayed at Munich until the morning of the 30th. When he got back to Croydon he stated: 'Peace has been won for a generation'.

From Paul Reynaud, *In the Thick of the Fight*, Flammarion et Cie, Paris

Questions

1 Who is the person portrayed in the cartoon?

2 What efforts had made Hitler grateful to Neville Chamberlain?

3 Suggest why Hitler made his 26 September speech. Who was meant to take notice of it? What difference could it have made if they had seen the secret Hossbach memorandum on page 7?

4 Does the cartoon suggest any reasons why people in Britain might be willing to believe what Hitler said?

5 Why do you think Hitler brought Czechoslovakia's other minorities (such as Poles, Slovaks and Ruthenes) into his speech?

6 Summarise the impression Reynaud gives about the feelings of the French after the signing. Why should they be different from the British?

6 A Jew in Berlin

This extract is taken from A Boy in Your Situation, *an autobiography by Charles Hannam published in 1977. He was born in Essen in 1925, the son of a wealthy Jewish banker, and was sent to Britain in 1939. His father disappeared under the Nazi rule and Karl Hartland became an Englishman – Charles Hannam.*

A   Raided by stormtroopers

He was fast asleep when the front doorbell rang. Not the usual ring but long, long rings that just went on. Karl jumped up and rushed downstairs. There was also a crashing sound from the back door. A group of stormtroopers pushed their way in.

'You the only one here?'

'No, there is also my grandfather.'

Grandfather Freudenberg appeared on the stairs. He too was fully dressed.

'Any weapons in the house?' they asked.

'We handed the air gun to the police,' Karl said.

He was thinking, what if they set the house on fire. Father is in the attic. If I tell them he is there they will kill him. The men were in brown uniforms and carried pistols and daggers. Their gun holsters, Karl noticed, were open. Karl heard a crashing sound from the kitchen. The men charged right up the stairs at great speed, a bit like Karl when he was pretending to be engaged in house-to-house fighting. There were crashes and bangs all over the place.

An officer came up to Karl. 'Show us around.' Karl used very polite language and behaved like a guide in a country house. 'This is the drawing room.' He saw to his horror that the men were turning out drawers. They just pulled them out, turned them over and everything fell on the floor. The book cupboard went over.

'We are looking for arms,' the officer explained. 'Where is the dog?' he went on, looking at the lead hanging from a hook in the dressing room.

'He has been sent away, honoured sir,' Grandfather said. He followed the men at a respectful distance.

There were crashes in the kitchen and noises in the dining room, but Karl followed the officer. 'This is the bedroom of my parents.' One of the men went up to a chest of drawers and pulled it open and cases of bandages and plasters fell out. 'Look at what these Jews have got,'

From Charles Hannam, *A Boy in Your Situation*, Andre Deutsch, 1977.

the storm trooper said. 'They wallow in everything and we have got nothing.' They rushed from room to room. Karl saw one trooper with his camera. That was too much. 'That's my camera.' The trooper turned on him and took his shirt and twisted it round so that it was tight round Karl's throat. 'Listen, Jew Boy, the stormtroopers don't steal.' Karl's knees went weak and there was nothing he could do. The man let him go, pushing him away. He had a round face and glittering eyes and Karl saw the embroidered numbers on the flashes very closely. He stomped away and Karl followed.

Questions

1. What evidence can you find in this extract that makes you feel it is based on real events?
2. Would you have reacted in the same way as Karl, who was thirteen at the time?
3. Imagine you are the SS officer writing a report for your superiors. Write out the report on the events described in the extract.
4. In what ways does an account such as this add to your understanding of the Nazi persecution of the Jews?
5. Both Charles Hannam and George Clare (see page 8) wrote about their childhood in Berlin and Vienna thirty years after the end of the war. Does this affect the value of their writing as historical evidence?

7 Summer 1939

In March 1939 Hitler broke his promises to Neville Chamberlain and took over the whole of Czechoslovakia. At the same time Nazi propaganda was encouraging Germans in Poland and the three Baltic States (see map, page 6) to press for the right to unite with Germany. In an effort to stop Hitler, British and French statesmen changed their policy from appeasement. They gave Poland a guarantee that they would fight Germany if Hitler invaded her. The key question was about the attitude of the USSR. Would she fight Hitler, or would she stay out of any war? Britain and France negotiated with the USSR but the talks broke down. Then in August 1939 the foreign ministers of Germany and the Soviet Union (Molotov and Ribbentrop) signed the Russo-German Pact. The public part said the USSR would stay out of any war which involved Hitler. That left him free to attack Poland. The secret part of the Pact agreed that Russia and Germany would divide Poland between them.

The cartoon (Source A) was drawn by David Low at the time the treaty was signed. Source B is from the diary of the Soviet minister, Khrushchev. He describes how Stalin was entertaining his ministers and guests at a hunting party, and outlines Soviet thinking about the Pact.

A A strange meeting

David Low's cartoon of the Nazi-Soviet Pact appeared in the Daily Mail, *September 1939.*

B Stalin and the Russo-German Pact

Anyway, we met for dinner at Stalin's that Sunday in August, 1939, and while the trophies of our hunt were being prepared for the table, Stalin told us that Ribbentrop had brought with him a draft of a friendship and nonaggression treaty which we had signed. Stalin seemed very pleased with himself. He said that when the English and French who were still in Moscow found out about the treaty the next day, they would immediately leave for home. The English and French representatives who came to Moscow to talk with Voroshilov didn't really want to join forces with us against Germany at all. Our discussions with them were fruitless. We knew that they weren't serious about an alliance with us and that their real goal was to incite Hitler against us. We were just as glad to see them leave.

That's how the Ribbentrop-Molotov Pact, as it was called in the West, came into being. We knew perfectly well that Hitler was trying to trick us with the treaty. I heard with my own ears how Stalin said, 'Of course it's all a game to see who can fool whom. I know what Hitler's up to. He thinks he's outsmarted me, but actually it's I who have tricked him!' Stalin told Voroshilov, Beria, myself, and some other members of the Politbureau that because of this treaty the war would pass us by for a while longer. We would be able to stay neutral and save our strength. Then we would see what happened.

From N. Khrushchev, *Khrushchev Remembers* (trans. S. Talbott), Andre Deutsch, 1971.

Questions

1 Look at the map of Europe in 1937 (on page 6) and list the lands gained by Germany up to March 1939.

2 What difference would the gains make to Germany's position in a war with Britain and France?

3 Why did the attitude of the USSR become the most important question in 1939?

4 Why did Stalin feel he had 'tricked' Hitler?

5 What had happened by the time David Low drew his cartoon?

6 Why does Low show Hitler and Stalin greeting each other with the words in the cartoon?

7 What do the greetings tell you about how unlikely the Nazi-Soviet Pact would have been some months earlier?

8 In what ways do the two sources agree with each other about the Nazi-Soviet Pact?

8 Hitler Youth 1939

This extract is taken from Hausfrau at War *by Else Wendel, a book of memories of life in Germany during the war. Here she recalls 1 September 1939, when Germany attacked Poland on the excuse that Poles mistreated Germans, especially in Danzig and the Polish corridor. The housewife Else Wendel was confused that Hitler had changed from peaceful to military methods, but Mr Wolter, her boss, argued that Hitler's policies were the only way to put right the unjust treatment of Germans at the Treaty of Versailles.*

The enthusiasm shown by German young people when they heard Hitler is illustrated in the picture (Source B) of a rally held at Nuremburg in 1938.

A A mother's fears

Mr Wolter said to me that morning, 'You want your sons to live, don't you? Well, how can they live if Germany is to be cramped up – ein Volk ohne Raum (a people without living room)? Twenty years after the Treaty of Versailles and we are still separated from our own people by the Polish corridor! Danzig is a German town. If the Poles won't give it back to us voluntarily, then, all right, we march in and take it .... It's all trash when they accuse Germany of being responsible for the first World War, and say we must be punished. They talk of freedom to us, but where is freedom when a big town like Danzig can't come back into its Fatherland? Do you seriously think we would have got the Rhineland back if we hadn't marched into it?; or Austria?; or Czechoslovakia?; and our Army?; and our rivers?; we have got our Army and no more foreign restrictions in our country.' He looked at me with a certain pity. 'But, of course, you women don't understand politics. My wife is just the same.'

Somehow I just had to answer back. 'But up till now Hitler has done everything peacefully. I do admire his foresight and diplomacy, as long as it means peace. But this is war!'

Mr Wolter commented. 'No need to worry at all. You take my word for it, this war against Poland will be just a Blitzkrieg. It will be over in a flash.'

From Else Wendel, *Hausfrau at War*, Odhams Press, 1957.

B   Hitler Youth and the Fuehrer

Hitler driving round the stadium at Nuremburg, September 1938.

Questions

1 What case does Mr Wolter make for Hitler's aggressive acts up to 1939?

2 What reasons did Mr Wolter give for the treatment of Germany at Versailles?

3 How many examples of Hitler's breaking of the Treaty of Versailles can you find in this extract?

4 Does Else Wendel's reply in the second paragraph explain anything about support for Hitler in the 1930s?

5 Why do you think young people responded so warmly to Hitler's policies?

6 Was the war against Poland 'over in a flash'?

7 Imagine you were one of Else Wendel's children. Write down what you might have said to your mother about Hitler.

Part 3

Britain alone

9 The 'Phoney War', 1939–40

The Poles had a large army but they were overwhelmed by the speed and power of the German attack. In Source A General Guderian describes a surprise visit by Hitler to his armies in Poland 5 September 1939. For six months after the conquest of Poland, land and air warfare in Europe virtually stopped except for the Russian war against Finland. The sense of waiting for something to happen is caught in Source B, an extract from Derek Robinson's novel Piece of Cake, *published in 1983. It tells the story of the RAF in France in the spring of 1940. Derek Robinson was born in 1934 and in this novel he is trying to catch the feel of the time and show how it might be different from the legend which has grown up.*

A   Blitzkrieg into Poland

During the drive we discussed at first the course of events in my corps area. Hitler asked about casualties. I gave him the latest figures that I had received, some one hundred and fifty dead and seven hundred wounded for all the four divisions under my command during the Battle of the Corridor. He was amazed at the smallness of these figures and contrasted them with the casualties of his own old regiment, the List Regiment, during the World War: on the first day of battle that one regiment alone had lost more than two thousand dead and wounded. I was able to show him that the smallness of our casualties in this battle against a tough and courageous enemy was primarily due to the effectiveness of our tanks. Tanks are a life-saving weapon. The men's belief in the superiority of their armoured equipment had been greatly strengthened by their success in the Corridor. The enemy had suffered the total destruction of between two and three infantry divisions and one cavalry brigade. Thousands of prisoners and hundreds of guns had fallen into our hands.

From Heinz Guderian, *Panzer Leader*, Michael Joseph, 1952.

B RAF in France, spring 1940

Rex had the grass tennis-courts mown and marked out, and Barton organised a tournament. The Russo-Finnish war ended, in Russia's favour. 'B' flight bagged a Heinkel. Britain and France sent an invasion fleet to neutral Norway but Hitler's forces landed there the day before it arrived. Germany overran Denmark too. Cattermole received a parcel containing six silk scarves and a bill, which he threw away. The weather suddenly became warm enough for swimming, and the pilots found a perfect pool in the stream that ran through the grounds. 'A' flight saw, for the first time, a formation of Messerschmitt 109 fighters but they were only testing the Allied defences and no contact was made. Himmler ordered a concentration camp built at Auschwitz in Poland. Swallows and housemartins streaked up and down the stream, hurdling the swimmers and gorging on insects. Both flights saw the Luftwaffe's new twin-engined fighter-bomber, the Me-110, but only at a distance. Mussolini told the US ambassador in Rome that Germany could not be defeated. Cattermole received an anxious letter from Stickwell, asking him to make Rex pay his bills. Belgium announced yet again that it was neutral. The weather was so fine that Micky Marriott had the grass on the aerodrome cut twice a week. It was going to be a hot summer.

From Derek Robinson, *Piece of Cake*, Hamish Hamilton, 1983.

Questions

1. What evidence is there from Guderian's account to suggest Hitler was surprised by the German success?

2. Why did Guderian believe that there had been so few German casualties?

3. Why do you think that fighting in Europe virtually stopped over the winter 1939–40?

4. How does Derek Robinson create the sense of time standing still for the pilots in France?

5. What hints does he give to suggest that the Germans had superior aircraft available in 1940?

6. Choose the clue which gives the strongest evidence that this passage was written a long time after 1940.

7. In what way does the date of writing affect its usefulness as historical evidence?

10 Blackout, barrage balloons and the Home Guard

At home in Britain people waited for the attack from the air. Source A describes the blackout arrangements as recounted by various people in War Begins at Home *published 1940. This was based on a collection of reports from 'Mass Observation': a way of building up an impression of feelings and opinions by talking to people in pubs and other places. Source B is a description of barrage balloons written by a journalist at the time, J. L. Hodson. The photograph shows the Home Guard as it desperately prepared to withstand invasion.*

A Blackout

A woman: 'There's no need for all this darkness.'
Pub manageress: 'Wasn't Tuesday an awful night? I couldn't see a thing because the rain got on my glasses, and what with the blackout I walked into the sandbags under the clock, just by there. I hurt my leg, and it isn't better yet. That's a week ago, and I haven't been out since. It makes you frightened to go out, doesn't it, in case you get hurt again?'

From T. Harrison and C. Madge, *War Begins at Home*, Chatto and Windus, 1940

B Barrage balloons

... shining silver in the sun, or turning pink or golden, or shades of blue in the varied lights from dawn to evening, their cable singing some kind of tune, maybe, in a high wind and, just occasionally, the balloon itself, if something has gone wrong, turning over and over like a playful porpoise or, again lashing about with the fury of a wounded whale.

From Angus Calder, *The People's War*, Jonathan Cape, 1969.

A barrage balloon in Birchfield's Park, Manchester, 18 June 1941.

C   The Home Guard

Some of the 250 men in Maidenhead's Home Guard, June 1940. They are using their lunch hour for training – many are still wearing their work overalls.

Questions

1 What do the people in A mean by 'the blackout'?

2 What evidence is there that the blackout was resented? Suggest reasons why it was disliked at this time.

3 How were barrage balloons intended to work as a defence against air attack?

4 What does the picture above tell you about the organisation and membership of the Home Guard?

5 In what way does it help to understand the importance of Britain's air defences?

11 Blitzkrieg 1940

'Blitzkrieg' is German for a 'lightning war' carried out by tanks and infantry moving on vehicles and motor-cycles. Britain and France clung to the defensive approach to war, based upon the experiences in the trenches 1914–18. In May 1940 they met 'blitzkrieg' when motorised German Panzer troops were sent by their commander Guderian through the Ardennes and on to the coast of Dunkirk. The French did not believe Guderian could reach the River Meuse in less than nine days. He reached it in two and the first Germans crossed at three o'clock on 13 May 1940. German tanks followed at dawn the next day and drove along open roads, brushing aside French resistance which was taken by surprise.

The picture shows the first troops crossing the river. The extract is taken from A Thousand Shall Fall *by Hans Habe, who served in the defeated French army. His book was published in 1941.*

A Fight for a village

Behind the tank German motor-cycles appeared. As the street was too narrow they formed on the pavement. Each cycle had a sidecar with two men in it. Each of them was armed with an automatic rifle. But they had not yet started to move. My brain throbbed with the tension. Something seemed to be flying through my temples. How many were they? Were we not alone? Alone with a few dead and the half-dead whose cries rent the air. We did not know. Any sound would have been more bearable than this silence in which you couldn't tell where your comrades were. Even the machine-gunners in the next room did not stir.

At last the motor-cyclists started. They emerged at the right and left of the armoured car. One of the two men on each motor-cycle held his automatic rifle upward, the other horizontally down the street. They fired without interruption. In less than a fraction of a minute they were in front of our house. At least fifteen of them arrived at the same time. I was half-crouching under a window. Saint-Brice bent forward. I saw that he was taking aim. I made ready to shoot. Saint-Brice pulled the trigger. I followed him immediately. The miracle occurred – my Remington went off! I reloaded in feverish haste Despite the infernal noise that was suddenly unleashed – motor-cycles, armoured cars, aeroplanes, bombs, machine-gun fire, rifles – I distinctly heard orders shouted in German. Somebody cried 'Rein ins Haus!' ('Into the house!') Simultaneously the pane splintered. They were firing at our window.

I crawled into the adjoining room for ammunition. A bullet whistled by me. Curious, I thought unconsciously, this shot cannot come from the street. Then I heard somebody saying beside me, 'Oh, les salauds!'

I crawled to the three men at the machine-gun. And then I saw what, for the first time, struck me with horror. In a window of one of the few undamaged houses in the opposite side of the street – the same

From Hans Habe, *A Thousand Shall Fall*, Harcourt Brace Co., 1941.

house under the gate of which I had been hidden a short time before – a machine-gun had been set in place. Behind the machine-gun a German steel helmet emerged and quickly disappeared. But the man could not disappear quickly enough; I saw his face. His eyes stared at me. It was probably only my imagination, but it seemed to me that I had never before seen more evil eyes. And though I had never feared all the terrifying things invented by man, I was afraid of this man. Cannon, shells, and bombs are not terrifying. Only man is terrifying.

B   Crossing the Meuse

Questions

1 How does the picture of German troops crossing the river Meuse show the speed at which the Germans advanced?

2 Why was it so important to the Germans to get troops across the river Meuse?

3 From the account describe the way in which the 'blitzkrieg' was organised.

4 What does the passage tell you about the French fighting strength?

5 Would you agree that: 'Only man is terrifying'?

12 Dunkirk

In May 1940 about 400,000 Allied troops were pinned against the coast of Flanders by Hitler's advancing tanks. Eleven days later 338,000 men had been evacuated from the beaches around Dunkirk. Source A is taken from an account called Return via Dunkirk *published in 1940. It tells the story of a gunner officer who took part in the evacuation. Britain expected invasion and Churchill was to say in the House of Commons after Dunkirk, 4 June, 1940: 'We shall fight on the beaches, we shall fight on the landing grounds, we shall fight in the fields and in the streets, we shall fight in the hills. We shall never surrender.'*

A   Return via Dunkirk

From the margin of the sea, at fairly wide intervals, three long thin black lines protruded into the water, conveying the effect of low wooden breakwater. These were lines of men, waiting in queues till boats arrived to transport them a score or so at a time, to the steamers and warships that were filling up with the last survivors. The queues stood there, fixed and almost as regular as if ruled. No bunching, no pushing. Nothing like the mix-up to be seen at the turnstiles when a crowd is going into a football match. Much more orderly, even, than a waiting theatre queue.

About this time, afraid that some of our men might be tailing off, I began shouting, '2004th Field Regiment . . . 2004th Field Regiment . . .'

A group of dead and dying soldiers on the path in front of us quickened our desire to quit the promenade. Stepping over the bodies we marched down the slope on to the dark beach. Dunkirk front was now a lurid study in red and black; flames, smoke, and the night itself all mingling together to compose a frightful panorama of death and destruction. Red and black, all the time, except for an occasional flash of white low in the sky miles away to the left and right where big shells from coastal defence guns at Calais and Nieuport were being hurled into the town.

Down on the beach you immediately felt yourself surrounded by a deadly evil atmosphere. A horrible stench of blood and mutilated flesh pervaded the place. There was no escape from it. Not a breath of air was blowing to dissipate the appalling odour that arose from the dead bodies that had been lying on the sand, in some cases for several days. We might have been walking through a slaughter-house on a hot day. The darkness, which hid some of the sights of horror from our eyes, seemed to thicken this dreadful stench. It created the impression that death was hovering around, very near at hand.

From Gun Buster, *Return via Dunkirk*, Hodder and Stoughton, 1940.

B The beach at Dunkirk

Questions

1 Which part of the extract most brings the scene at Dunkirk alive to you?

2 Why did this officer shout: '2004th Field Regiment'?

3 What can you learn from this account about the organisation of the evacuation?

4 Read Churchill's words to the House of Commons again. What do you think is meant by the 'Dunkirk spirit'?

5 Study the photograph carefully and then read the account by the British gunnery officer again. How far do you think that description is supported by the picture?

6 Imagine you were on the beach at Dunkirk. Write an account of your feelings as you waited to be taken off by sea.

13 Battle of Britain

The battle of Britain was fought in the summer sky over Southern England during the months of August and September 1940. The German airforce intended to smash British resistance and in the first weeks tried to destroy RAF airfields. Later they began to bomb cities. Five hundred and ten fighter pilots and air gunners were killed in the Battle. One was Richard Hillary, whose book The Last Enemy *was published in 1941 after his death. Source B is from* Wing Leader *by Johnnie Johnson, a pilot who survived. His book was published in 1956.*

A   The last enemy

I looked down. It was a completely cloudless sky and way below lay the English countryside, stretching lazily into the distance a quite extraordinary picture of green and purple in the setting sun.

I took a glance at my altimeter. We were at twenty-eight thousand feet [850 metres]. At that moment Sheep yelled 'Tally-ho' and dropped down in front of Uncle George in a slow dive in the direction of the approaching planes. Uncle George saw them at once.

'O.K. Line astern.'

I drew in behind Stapme and took a look at them. They were about two thousand feet [600 metres] below us, which was a pleasant change, but they must have spotted us at the same moment, for they were forming a protective circle, one behind the other, which is a defence formation hard to break.

'Echelon starboard', came Uncle George's voice.

We spread out fanwise to the right.

'Going down!'

One after the other we peeled off in a power dive. I picked out one machine and switched my gun-button to 'Fire'. At three hundred yards [275 metres] I had him in my sights. At two hundred I opened up in a long four-second burst and saw the tracer going into his nose. Then I was pulling out, so hard that I could feel my eyes dropping through my neck. Coming round in a slow climbing turn, I saw that we had broken them up. The sky was now a mass of individual dog-fights. Several of them had already been knocked down. One I hoped was mine, but on pulling up I had not been able to see the result. To my left I saw Peter Pease making a head-on attack on a Messerschmitt. They were headed straight for each other and it looked as though the Messerschmitt pulled up, taking Peter's fire full in the belly. It rolled on to its back, yellow flames pouring from the cockpit, and vanished.

From R. Hillary, *The Last Enemy*, Macmillan, 1942.

B Wing leader

Throughout it all the radio is never silent – shouts, oaths, exhortations and terse commands. You single out an opponent. Jockey for position. All clear behind! The bullets from your eight guns go pumping into his belly. He begins to smoke. But the wicked tracer sparkles and flashes over the top of your own cockpit and you break into a tight turn. Now you have two enemies. The 109 on your tail and your remorseless, ever-present opponent 'G', the force of gravity. Over your shoulder you can still see the ugly, questing snout of the 109. You tighten the turn. The Spit protests and shudders, and when the blood drains from your eyes you 'grey-out'. But you keep turning, for life itself is the stake. And now your blood feels like molten lead and runs from head to legs. You black out! And you ease the turn to recover in a grey, unreal world of spinning horizons. Cautiously you climb into the sun. You have lost too much height and your opponent has gone – disappeared. You are completely alone in your own bit of sky, bounded by the blue vault above and the coloured drapery of earth below.

From J. Johnson, *Wing Leader*, Chatto and Windus, 1956.

Questions

1 Explain the terms: altimeter, dog-fights, echelon, tracer, 'G' force.

2 What were: Messerschmitt 109 and 'Spits'? What other aircraft were used during the Battle of Britain?

3 Are there any differences in the accounts which might be due to the fact that one was written a few months after the battle and the other after sixteen years?

4 Write down the impression of fighter combat you have gained from these extracts.

14 'Blitz'

On 24 August 1940 a flight of German bombers lost their way and dropped bombs on homes in London. The next day the British retaliated by bombing Berlin. Hitler then ordered his planes to make an all out attack on cities instead of airfields. The 'blitz' started on 7 September 1940. By December, 1941 nearly 30,000 civilians were killed in the 'blitz' and three and a half million homes had been damaged or destroyed.

Richard Hillary, the fighter pilot, was in London recovering from injuries gained in the Battle of Britain. In this extract from The Last Enemy *he describes how he discovered what bombing meant to civilians. Henry Moore, the sculptor and artist, visited underground stations in London, making sketches of people sheltering from the raids. The sketches were worked up into official pictures, to give an artist's record of the shelters during the 'blitz'.*

A   On the receiving end of bombs

My hands were tight-pressed over my ears but the detonation deafened me. The floor rose up and smashed against my face, the swing-door tore off its hinges and crashed over a table, glass splinters flew across the room, and behind the bar every bottle in the place seemed to be breaking. The lights went out but there was no darkness. An orange glow from across the street shone through the wall and threw everything into a strong relief.

I scrambled unsteadily to my feet and was leaning over the bar to see what had happened to the unfortunate barmaid when a voice said 'Anyone hurt?' and there was an AFS man shining a torch. At that everyone began to move, but slowly and reluctantly as though coming out of a dream. The girl stood white and shaken in a corner, her arm about her companion, but she was unhurt and had stopped talking. Only the barmaid failed to get up.

'I think there is someone hurt behind the bar,' I said. The fireman nodded and went out, to return almost immediately with two stretcher-bearers who made a cursory inspection and discovered that she had escaped with no more than a severe cut on the head. They got her on to the stretcher and disappeared.

Together with the man in the AFS, the taxi-driver and I found our way out into the street. He turned to us almost apologetically. 'If you have nothing very urgent on hand,' he said, 'I wonder if you'd help here for a bit. You see it was the house next to you that was hit, and there's someone buried in there.'

I turned and looked on a heap of bricks and mortar, wooden beams and doors, and one framed picture unbroken. It was the first time that I had seen a building newly blasted. Often had I left the flat in the morning and walked up Piccadilly, aware vaguely of the ominously tidy gap between two houses, but further my mind had not gone.

From R. Hillary, *The Last Enemy*, Macmillan, 1942.

B Underground shelter

Henry Moore's record of people sheltering during the 'blitz'.

Questions

1. What created 'the orange glow from across the street'?

2. Describe the job done by the AFS.

3. What did Hillary understand about the effect of bombing which he had not realised before?

4. Does the passage give any evidence about how Londoners reacted to the 'blitz'?

5. Henry Moore said the war made him aware of 'life itself'. How far do you think this picture gives an accurate idea of people sheltering from the bombing?

6. Do you think war artists or war photographers produce the most useful evidence for studying history?

Part 4

Worldwide war 1941

15 War at sea

Britain as an island depended upon supplies by sea. Her lifeline was made up of convoys of merchant ships protected by the Royal Navy. This lifeline was always in danger of attack from German submarines. Heinz Schaeffer wrote his account of German submarine warfare in U-Boat 977, *published in 1952. This extract describes an attack on a tanker, after the first hit has just been scored. The National Savings Committee poster was produced in 1941.*

A   Attack on a tanker

Her wireless is still working, however. An SOS goes out on the six hundred-metre wavelength. German submarine – with our position.

'Very good', remarks the chief quartermaster, 'it's friendly of the English to give us an exact position. No more need to worry to-day.'

She's no longer moving through the water and is giving off steam. Rudder and steering apparatus seem to be damaged. We attack again. It's easy now, for we are just over a thousand metres away. They've spotted our periscope, though, and with all their machine-guns and quick-firers let fly at us, endangering the periscope glass. We attack from the other quarter and dive under the ship at ten fathoms. The hydrophone-operator reports:

'She's right overhead!'

In a submarine attack the Commander controls the ship, gives the target information and fires the torpedoes himself. The torpedo-officer only sees that the proper settings are put on the attack-table. This time we are going to fire the stern tube, which we don't often get the chance to use.

'Range four hundred metres . . . fire!'

The roar's terrific. We've fired from much closer this time; underwater the noise is frightful. The tanker has broken in two.

Everyone has a look through the periscope. The fine ship before us is sinking into the sea. Emotion overcomes us. The daemonic madness of destruction that becomes law the moment a war breaks out has us in its grip. Under its spell as we are, what else can we do? Lifeboats and rafts are meanwhile being lowered, those aboard saving themselves as best they may. We can't help without running into grave danger, and in any case we've no room aboard – U-boats are built to allow space for the ship's company and no more. The enemy is well equipped with life-saving gear and these men on the tanker will certainly soon be picked up by a warship.

From Heinz Schaeffer, *U-Boat 977*, William Kimber, 1952.

B Save for the brave

Questions

1 What did the quartermaster mean by his joking remark in the second paragraph of extract A?

2 Explain what a periscope and a hydrophone are.

3 Why do you think the Germans did not often get the chance to use the stern tubes?

4 Does the last paragraph suggest that the writer was at all sad to see the tanker sink?

5 Why could the U-boat not pick up survivors?

6 From the extract what can you learn about the protection merchant ships had against submarines?

7 What was meant by the Kitchen front?

8 What does this poster show about the importance of Britain's merchant ships?

9 Write a letter to a merchant seaman telling him how important you feel his work to be if the war is to be won.

16 Lease-lend

Many people in the United States wished their country to remain in isolation out of any involvement in war. President Roosevelt was aware of this which made him concerned about the failure of the League of Nations which had been set up to settle quarrels between states. He explained his worries in a speech to the American people in October 1937 (Source A). In 1940 American opinion was still divided about helping Britain, who stood alone against Hitler. Roosevelt won the presidential election in 1940 and was in the White House for a third time. A few weeks after the election, on 17 December, he announced his plans for 'lease-lend' to the press (Source B).

A F. D. Roosevelt on the League, 1937

How happy we are that the circumstances of the moment permit us to put our money into bridges and boulevards, dams and reforestation, the conservation of our soil and many other kinds of useful works rather than into huge standing armies and vast supplies of implements of war.

I am compelled and you are compelled, nevertheless, to look ahead. The peace, the freedom and the security of ninety per cent of the population of the world is being jeopardized by the remaining ten per cent who are threatening a breakdown of all international order and law. Surely the ninety per cent who want to live in peace under law and in accordance with moral standards that have received almost universal acceptance through the centuries, can and must find some way to make their will prevail ...

It seems to be unfortunately true that the epidemic of world lawlessness is spreading.

When an epidemic of physical disease starts to spread, the community approves and joins in a quarantine of the patients in order to protect the health of the community against the spread of the disease.

From T. P. Brocknay, *Basic Documents in United States Foreign Policy*, Van Nostrand, 1957.

B F. D. Roosevelt on lease-lend, 1940

Well, let me give you an illustration. Suppose my neighbour's home catches fire and I have a length of garden hose four or five hundred feet [120–150 metres] away. If he can take my garden hose and connect it up with his hydrant, I may help him to put out his fire. Now, what do I do? I don't say to him before that operation, 'Neighbour, my garden hose cost me $15; you have to pay me $15 for it' – I want my garden hose back after the fire is over. All right. If it goes through the fire all right, intact, without any damage to it, he gives it back to me and thanks me very much for the use of it. But suppose it gets smashed up – holes in it – during the fire; we don't have to have too much formality about it, but I say to him 'I was glad to lend you that hose; I see I can't use it any more, it's all smashed up.' He says, 'How many feet of it were there?' I tell him, 'There were a hundred and fifty feet of it.' He says, 'All right, I will replace it.' Now, if I get a nice garden hose back, I am in pretty good shape. In other words, if you lend certain munitions and get the munitions back at the end of the war, if they are intact – haven't been hurt – you are all right.

From D. Flower and J. Reeves, *The War 1939–45*, Cassell, 1960.

Questions

1. What name is given to the schemes that Roosevelt mentions in the first paragraph in Source A?
2. Suggest examples of the ten per cent who were threatening international law and order in the 1930s.
3. Why should their behaviour compel Roosevelt and the American people to look ahead?
4. What can you learn from the fact that Roosevelt has to persuade the American people to accept the idea of lease-lend?
5. Is the metaphor of the garden hose a good one?
6. Why was lease-lend so important to Britain in 1940?
7. Do you think Roosevelt really expected to get munitions back?
8. Give as many reasons as you can for opposition to lease-lend in the United States.

17 Hitler's plans and Fortress Europe

Hitler outlined his plans for conquering Eastern Europe in December 1940 (Source A). By invading the USSR he planned to create a slave empire to support his master-race. In 1940 Hans Franck was appointed Governor-General of Poland and Source B is part of his statement to the government in Cracow on 16 December 1941. Picture C shows orphans in Warsaw for whom nobody cared.

A Hitler on the Soviet Union, 1940

The German armed forces must be prepared to crush Soviet Russia in a quick campaign before the end of the war against England (case 'Barbarossa').

For this purpose the army will have to employ all available units with the reservation that the occupied territories will have to be safeguarded against surprise attacks.

For the Eastern campaign the air force will have to free such strong forces for the support of the army that a quick completion of the ground operations may be expected and that damage of the Eastern German territories will be avoided as much as possible. This concentration of the main effort in the East is limited by the following reservation: that the entire battle against enemy air attacks and that the attacks on England and especially the supply for them must not be permitted to break down.

Concentration of the main effort of the navy remains unequivocally against England also during an Eastern campaign.

From *Trial of German War Criminals*, HMSO, 1946.

B Hans Franck previews the 'final solution'

We too find the Jews exceptionally troublesome animals. We have about two and a half million Jews in the territory. If we include those inter-married with Jews and so on, the total is about three and a half millions. We can't shoot three and a half million Jews, nor can we poison them, but we shall be able to take measures of some kind finally to liquidate them, probably bound up with the more comprehensive measures to be discussed with the Reich government.

From E. Leiser, *Pictorial History of Nazi Germany*, Penguin, 1962.

C Orphans in Warsaw

A German soldier herds orphaned children out of the Warsaw ghetto, 1941

Questions

1 What was the codename for the German invasion of Russia?

2 With the help of a map explain what the leaders of the German army, navy and air force would have to do to carry out Hitler's orders.

3 Which were the occupied territories at this time?

4 What can you learn from the first sentence in B?

5 Hans Franck hints at a 'final solution' to liquidating the Jews. What was it?

6 Is the photograph effective in creating an impression of fear and despair?

18 Barbarossa

German forces began 'Operation Barbarossa' with an attack along the length of the Russian frontier on 22 June 1941. In this massive 'blitzkrieg' Hitler's armies reached the outskirts of Leningrad on 8 September 1941, and began a siege of the city which lasted for 900 days. A. Fadeyer gives one recollection of the suffering in Leningrad in Source B from Leningrad in the Days of the Blockade, *published 1946. By 2 December 1941 the Germans were on the edge of Moscow, when the Russian winter closed in. Source C tells what that meant, through the account written by Heinrich Haape, a medical officer with the German army, in his book* Moscow Tram Stop *published in 1957. On 6 December the Russians counter-attacked and pushed the Germans two hundred kilometres back from Moscow. Heinrich Haape's second extract is after this counter-attack as the winter cold set in.*

A   The German invasion of the USSR

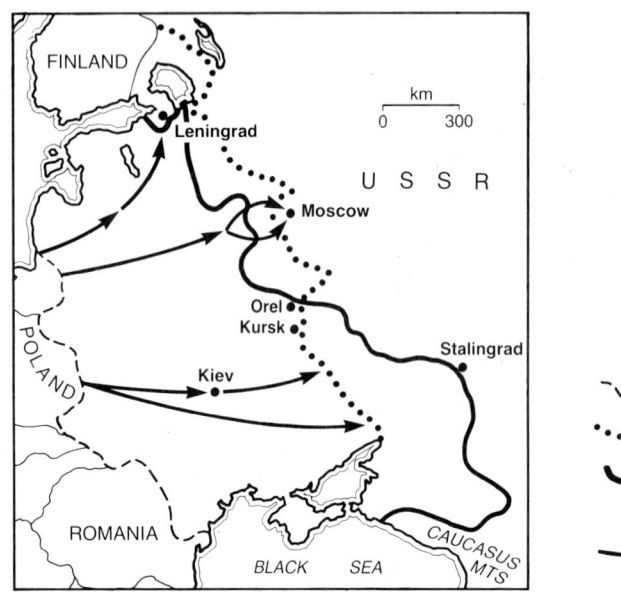

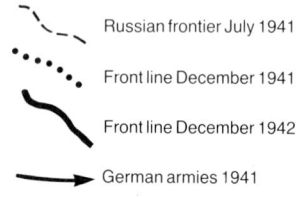

B   Besieged in Leningrad

When I entered the room my cousin, who had a friend with her, a woman as emaciated as herself, was having her dinner. Because of the increased rations for the First of May, their dinner, judged by Leningrad standards, might have been called luxurious. It included even beer and vodka prepared from dried orange rind. Among the dishes was the famous Leningrad-blockade jelly – a jelly made from carpenter's glue. Here was the reverse process: you cooked the glue, removed all the bone scum – or rather, the scum of what had once been bone – and added gelatine to the rest. Then you let it cool.

From A. Fadeyer, *Leningrad in the Days of the Blockade*, Hutchinson, 1946.

C Fighting the Russian winter

We walked silently down the road to the stone shed. There was not a movement around us as we stopped and stared at the wooden seats on which thousands of Muscovites had sat and waited for the tram to clang down the road from Moscow. There was an old wooden bin attached to one wall. I felt inside and dragged out a handful of old tram tickets. We picked out the cyrillic letters, which by now we knew spelled Moscow.

Slowly we trudged back to the car. Kageneck broke the silence and spoke for both of us: 'It must fall, yet . . . I wonder . . .'

Fischer turned the car round and we headed back along the white road.

The snow was falling a little more heavily now. . . .

Now we had an opportunity to equip our men with more winter clothing. Kageneck ordered that the seventy-three dead Russians be carried to the village and stripped of their felt-lined boots and warm clothing.

But the bodies were frozen stiff. And those invaluable boots were frozen to the Russians' legs.

'Saw their legs off', ordered Kageneck.

The men hacked off the dead men's legs below the knee and put legs, with boots still attached, into the ovens. Within ten or fifteen minutes the legs were sufficiently thawed for the soldiers to strip off the vital boots.

From H. Haape, *Moscow Tram Stop*, Collins, 1957.

Questions

1. Does the map suggest any reason why the Germans had early successes against the Russian defences?

2. In what way might not starting Barbarossa until 22 June have made a difference to its success?

3. Suggest reasons why the Germans settled down to besiege Leningrad instead of trying to capture it in 1940.

4. Suggest a reason why Leningrad rations were increased for 1 May 1941.

5. Try to invent some dishes, such as Leningrad jelly, to be eaten under siege conditions.

6. What evidence is there in the first extract of Source C that the Germans were close to Moscow centre?

7. Does the rest of the writing in the first extract of Source C suggest any reasons for Kageneck to wonder whether Moscow would fall?

8. What evidence is there in the second extract of Source C, about the effects of the cold on the German offensive in Russia?

19 Desert war

The only major British success up to February 1941 had been in North Africa. British armies had defeated Italian forces, who were trying to drive them out of Egypt and take the Suez Canal, which was vital for oil supplies. In February 1941 Hitler sent General Erwin Rommel with the 'Afrika Korps' to help the Italians. Rommel's troops and the British fought a duel across the North African desert. This extract from Lieutenant Heinz Werner Schmidt's book With Rommel in the Desert, *1951, catches the desert atmosphere and the way in which battles swung back and forth. Here he describes a pause after a British tank group had been driven away. Photograph B shows tanks in the Egyptian desert in August 1942.*

A After a battle

Firing had ceased. After perhaps a quarter of an hour I heard the tanks rolling off towards the south. Silence descended on the battlefield. But I still lay there like a sleeping man.

When I lifted my head the sky had dimmed from its brassy afternoon glare. Evening was coming. I saw no sign of life all round. Then I was startled by a figure that burst like a jack-in-the box from a slit-trench some way back. It was my man Muller.

He had an anguished expression on his face. 'Are you well, Herr Oberleutnant?' he called to me. And he added oddly, 'I am not'.

'Get down here,' I ordered Muller. 'We shall wait until it is dark before we move.'

'Herr Oberleutnant,' said Muller, 'that venison was just ready when the Tommies came.'

As soon as darkness had fallen on the battlefield Muller led me back to the wadi, where the gazelle had been roasted. A haunch, still warm, lay on a sheet of iron there. Muller's flask still held coffee. We tore off hunks of the tasty but exceedingly tough meat and swallowed it.

I can still remember the feeling of the juice running down from the corners of my mouth. It was good to be alive. That sense of futility and the inevitability of death that had overwhelmed me in the slit-trench had gone. The will to live is strong in us.

From Heinz Werner Schmidt, *With Rommel in the Desert*, Harrap, 1951.

B Tank warfare in the desert

British tanks, led by General Grant, in battle order in the Western desert, 17 February 1942.

Questions

1 Why did Schmidt wait until dark before moving?

2 What information is given by the fact that the haunch of venison and flask of coffee were still in place when the British moved?

3 Write the story of the battle of Source A as the British tank commander might have written it.

4 List the difficulties of fighting over ground as shown in the picture.

5 What objectives would a desert group try to capture?

20 The Far East

The Japanese had conquered Eastern China by 1939 and were poised to take control of South-East Asia, where most territories were ruled and defended by Britain, France and Holland. They saw their chance in 1940 with the defeat of France and Holland and the expected collapse of Britain. They signed a pact with Italy and Germany in September 1940, and prepared to surprise the only power standing in their way with its powerful navy, the USA. The similarity of style of government in Japan and Germany is described by J. Gunther in his book Inside Asia *published in 1939.*

A Japanese expansion in the Far East

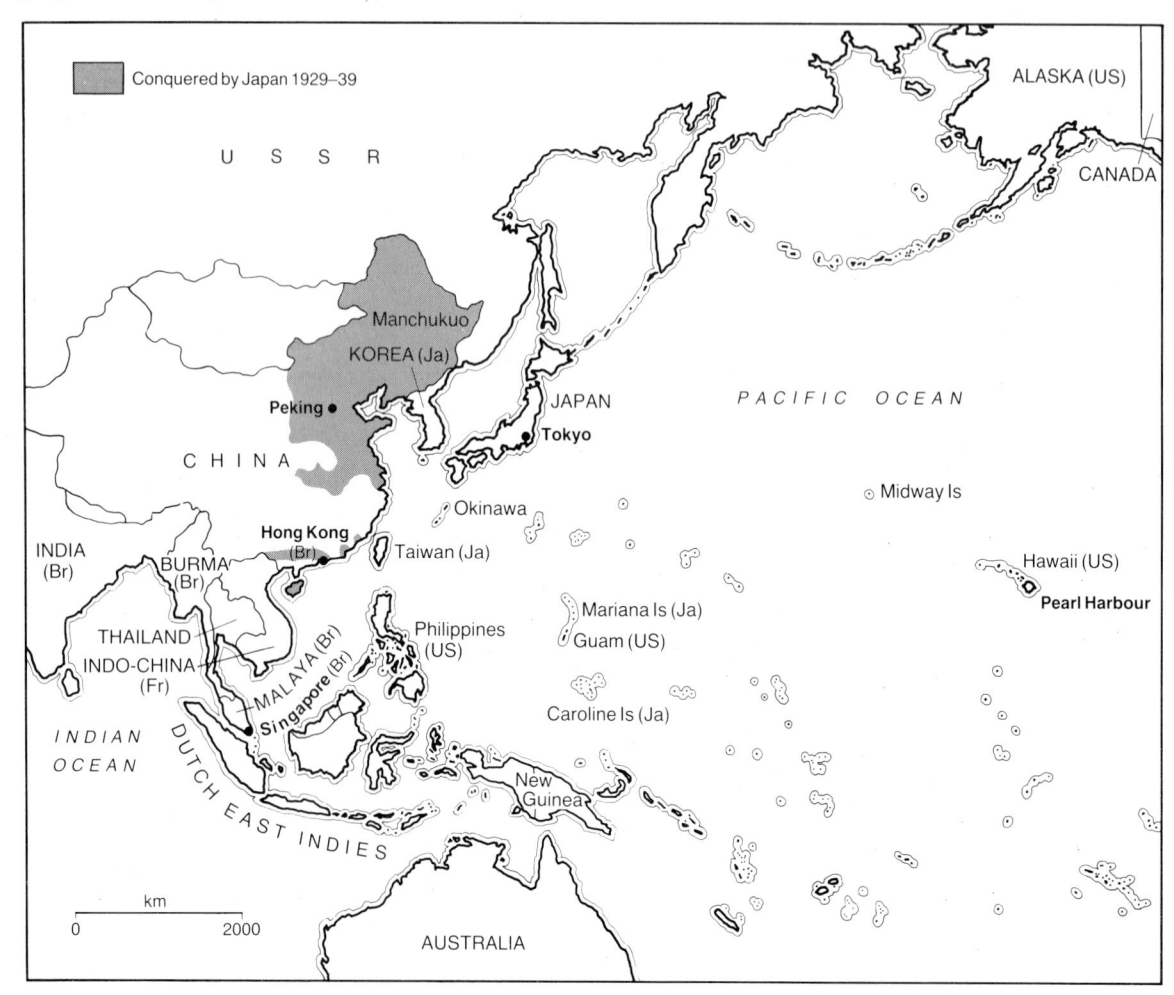

40

B Links between Japan and Germany

Japan and Germany at least have strong community of interest. Both countries believe in race, and Japan has begun to flirt with anti-Semitism; both are expansionist states, which were once put in the 'have-not' category; both fear and dislike the USSR on nationalist grounds. Japan borrowed its constitution from a German model, and built its schools and trained its army with German methods. In Japan, conversely, I felt that I was beginning to understand something of Nazi religious impulses and ideas. Worship of the state, with Hitler as its prophet, is strikingly like Shinto and Emperor-worship in Japan. In 1938 a 'culture accord' was signed between Japan and Germany, and one of its first results – though one would not normally put it in the culture classification – was complete publication of *Mein Kampf* in Japanese. As regards economics, Japanese-German collaboration has amounted to little, since Japan above all wants credit, a commodity which neither Germany – nor Italy, the other ally – can export.

From J. Gunther, *Inside Asia*, Harper, 1939.

Questions

1 Use the map to explain which powers were common enemies of Germany and Japan.

2 John Gunther gives six examples of similarities between Germany and Japan. Make notes in two columns to explain what they were.

3 Explain what Japan wanted which Germany and Italy couldn't supply.

4 What kind of warfare would be fought in this area of the world?

5 Write a letter home from Hong Kong in 1939 describing your fears for the future.

21 Japan strikes: Pearl Harbour

Japan launched her attack by sea and air on Pearl Harbour (see map on page 41) on 7 December 1941, which Roosevelt called the 'day of infamy'. Source A is taken from Day of Infamy *by Walter Lord. It was published in 1957 and based upon careful research. Walter Lord talked and corresponded with 577 people who were present at Pearl Harbour. He interviewed Japanese commanders and spent weeks in Hawaii going over each of the bases attacked. This extract shows how stunned the men on the American warships were by the Japanese attack.*

After the attack the Japanese were then able to sweep over British, French, Dutch and American territories in South-East Asia. They moved with speed on Singapore and landed in the Philippine Islands. Source B is an account of the retreat from the capital of the Philippines, Manila. It is taken from Retreat, Hell! *written in 1944 by William Martin Camp, a member of the US medical corps.*

A Day of infamy

Worst of all was the *Oklahoma*. The second torpedo put out her lights; the next three ripped open what was left of her port side. The sea swirled in, driving Seaman George Murphy from his post in the print shop on third deck as soon as he got there. His group retreated midships, slamming a watertight door behind them. The list grew steeper, and within seconds the water was squirting around the seams, filling that compartment too. As the ship heeled further, Chief Yeoman George Smith shifted over to a starboard ladder to reach his battle station. Everybody else had the same idea. In the flicker of a few emergency lamps men pushed and shoved, trying to climb over and around each other on the few usable ladders. It was a dark, sweat-smeared nightmare.

No matter how bad things were, men remembered to take care of absurd details. Radioman Robert Gamble of the *Tennessee* ignored the old shoes beside his bunk, went to his locker, and carefully put on a brand-new pair to start the war right. The *Nevada* musicians put their instruments away before going to their stations. (Exception – one man took along his cornet and excitedly threw it into a shell hoist along with some shells for the anti-aircraft guns above.)

From Walter Lord, *Day of Infamy*, Henry Holt and Co., 1957.

B Retreat from Manila

The road to Manila was once a broad four-laned highway of concrete pan macadam, hard and smooth, but the dust from fallen buildings and great clouds of dirt had descended upon it in a thin layer which was stirred up as we rolled along in the heavy convoy. The road was crowded with refugees loaded in automobiles, 'carabao'-drawn carts, 'carranatas', push-carts with heavy wooden wheels, wagons and all kinds of vehicles from the primitive farm carts to modern limousines. Those who lived in Manila were swarming to get out of the city, and country people were streaming into it, hoping to find safety there from the bombs.

In the light of the fires I could see on every face that drawn, terrified look, the same expression I recalled on the faces of the Chinese who had streamed into the International Settlement of Shanghai when the Japs bombed their homes and destroyed their towns. In every vehicle were the same things – blankets, chairs, boxes. Bundles of clothing and cooking utensils were tied up in sheets and blankets. Some of the wealthier families had mattresses piled upon the tops of their cars, with favourite chairs or tables or bicycles lashed to the rear. In the carts and wagons of the poor were chairs, tables, copper kettles, oil stoves, blankets and bundles of clothing. The poor were taking everything they owned, but the rich were leaving all but a few treasures behind.

From W. M. Camp, *Retreat, Hell!* Constable, 1944.

Questions

1. What evidence is there is Walter Lord's account for complete surprise?

2. Describe in your own words what was happening to the *Oklahoma*.

3. What problems would Walter Lord have had in putting together a truthful story of Pearl Harbour?

4. Can you account for the way in which men took care of 'absurd details'?

5. What evidence is there in Camp's account for the complete success of the Japanese attack?

6. With whom do you think William Camp particularly sympathises in this situation?

Part 5

The tide turns 1942–3

22 Stalingrad

In the summer of 1942 Hitler's Panzers advanced on the Volga in a drive south to the Caspian Sea and the Soviet oilfields. Hitler ordered them to capture Stalingrad rather than go round it, but the Russians defended the city building by building. The photograph of the suburbs was taken by Georgi Zelona, one of a team of Soviet press photographers with the front line troops. The Germans met not only savage fighting but also forty-four degrees of frost. By the end of 1942 they were pinned down in Stalingrad while Soviet forces outside the town attacked on all sides. Hitler ordered his forces to fight on to the last man and the last round. The letter from a German soldier in Stalingrad is from Last Letters from Stalingrad *published in 1956. This is a collection made from the letters sent by the surrounded German forces.*

A Fighting in Stalingrad

B Letter from Stalingrad

My hands are done for, and have been ever since the beginning of December. The little finger of my left hand is missing and – what's even worse – the three middle fingers of my right one are frozen. I can only hold my mug with my thumb and little finger. I'm pretty helpless; only when a man has lost any fingers does he see how much he needs them for the very smallest jobs. The best thing I can do with the little finger is to shoot with it. My hands are finished. After all, even if I'm not fit for anything else, I can't go on shooting for the rest of my life. Or would I still make a gamekeeper, I wonder? That's a pretty grim kind of humour, I know. The only reason I write such things is to keep my nerves steady.

A week ago Kurt Hahnke – you may remember him from the lectures we attended in '37 – played the Appassionata on a grand piano in a little side street by the Red Square. Not a thing one sees every day of the week – a grand piano planted in the middle of a street. The house it came from had to be demolished, but I suppose they took pity on the piano and fetched it out beforehand. Every private soldier who passed that way had thumped around on it: where else I ask you, would you find pianos standing out in the street?

From *Last Letters from Stalingrad*, Methuen, 1956.

Questions

1 What sort of fighting is shown in the photograph?

2 What evidence does it give you about the difficulties faced by the Panzers?

3 Do you think this is an effective war photograph?

4 What does the soldier's account of his frostbite suggest about the state of the German army in Stalingrad?

5 Suggest why the house that held the piano had to be demolished.

6 If you came across the piano, what might you think it symbolised?

23 Kursk and the Russian advance

Hitler was determined to make up in the summer of 1943 what he had lost in the winter at Stalingrad. In 1942 the Russians had produced more than double the German output of tanks. When a vast force of German tanks attacked at Kursk on 5 July 1963 (see map on page 36) the Russians were overjoyed that 586 were crippled or destroyed on the first day. Source A is from the historian John Erickson's The Road to Berlin, 1983, and is an historian's view of this battle. The effect on Russian morale was great and the Red Army went on the offensive. Moscow Radio's star announcer, Levitan, began a series of 'victory salutes' (B) with the announcement of the capture of the cities of Orel and Belgorod on 5 August 1943. There were to be over 300 of these salutes before final victory. Max Alpert was one of the pioneers of Soviet photography and was a war correspondent with the Soviet Army as they began the advance against the Germans. His photograph (C) of his battalion commander, A. G. Yeryomenko, became a symbol of the Russian counter-attack.

A Kursk 5–6 July 1943

Within twelve hours both sides were furiously stoking the great glowing furnace of the battle for Kursk. The armour continued to mass and move on a scale unlike anything seen anywhere else in the war. Both commands watched this fiery escalation with grim, numbed fascination: German officers had never seen so many Soviet aircraft, while Soviet commanders – who had seen a lot – had never before seen such formidable massing of German tanks, all blotched in their green and yellow camouflage. These were tank armadas on the move, coming on in great squadrons of 100 and 200 machines or more, a score of Tigers and Ferdinand assault guns in the first echelon, groups of 50–60 medium tanks in the second and then the infantry screened by the armour. Now that Soviet tank armies were moving up into the main defensive fields, almost 4000 Soviet tanks and nearly 3000 German tanks and assault guns were being steadily drawn into this gigantic battle, which roared on hour after hour leaving ever-greater heaps of the dead and the dying, clumps of blazing or disabled armour, shattered personnel carriers and lorries, thickening columns of smoke coiling over the steppe. With each hour also, the traffic in mangled, twisted men brought to steaming, blood-soaked forward dressing stations continued to swell. The Russian *svodka*, the communiqué on the first day's fighting, revealed the scale of operations in its mammoth total of reported German tank losses: 'During the course of the day [5 July], 586 tanks were destroyed or put out of action.'

From John Erickson, *The Road to Berlin*, Weidenfeld and Nicolson, 1983.

B   Moscow Radio announcement 5 August 1943

Tonight at twenty-four o'clock, on August 5, the capital of our country, Moscow, will salute the valiant troops that liberated Orel and Belgorod with twelve artillery salvoes from 120 guns. I express my thanks to all the troops that took part in the offensive . . . Eternal glory to the heroes who fell in the struggle for the freedom of our country. Death to the German invaders.

From A. Werth, *Russia at War 1941–45*, Barrie Books Ltd, 1964.

C   Russian counter-attack

Questions

1 Why did both commands watch the battle with 'grim numbed fascination'?

2 In what ways does extract A show how historians can build up the feel of an important past event forty years later?

3 What does the radio announcement tell you about the Russian morale in 1943?

4 Why did the Russians regard the battle of Kursk as crucial?

5 The Russians regarded this battle as a turning point as the programme of 'victory salutes' showed. Do you agree?

6 Why is the picture of Alpert's combat commander so effective?

7 Would it have been so effective in a time of defeat?

24 El Alamein

In August 1942 the British Eighth Army had been driven back by Rommel's troops to Egypt and held a defensive line at El Alamein only 80 kilometres from Cairo. General Montgomery was placed in command of the Eighth Army and carefully built up his forces. He ordered them to attack on the night of 23 October 1942. After bitter fighting and the loss of many tanks the Eighth Army forced the Afrika Korps to retreat westwards. The map shows how North Africa was rapidly cleared of Axis troops. Source B is taken from The Black Watch and the King's Enemies *by Bernard Fergusson, published in 1950, and is an eyewitness account of the regiment.*

A   Allied advances in North Africa and Italy 1942–5

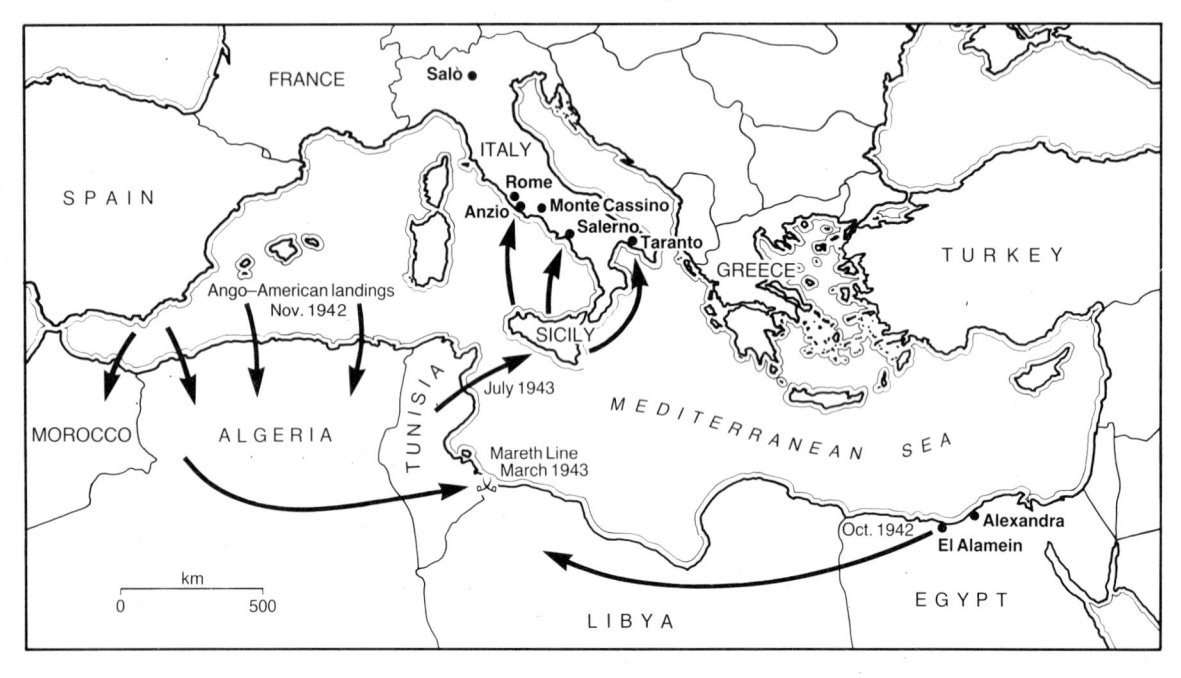

B Pursuit across the desert after El Alamein

Reveille would be at 5.30 a.m.; at six would come the order 'prepare to Move'; five minutes later 'Move'. A dim red light glowed on the Navigator's vehicle, and the rest would follow it. Soon there would be a little light; at 7.15 a.m. the chilly sun would pop into the sky; then there would be a halt, and the order 'Brew up!' A hundred little petrol fires would spring into being, and there would be a delicious breakfast of sausages, bacon, biscuits, marmalade and tea. While it was preparing, everyone would wash and shave in a mugful of water each. Off again, faster now with the advantage of daylight, the morning still crisp like a woodcock day at home, the Battalion's vehicles fanning out wide, now that they could see each other; halt and brew-up at noon, halt and brew-up again just before dark; and then five miles [8 kilometres] on a slightly different course, in case the enemy might make an intelligent guess at the location of the laager. Then the Navigator would flash 'Halt!' on his red light, the convoy would pull up, everyone would climb stiffly from his place, his face rigid with its mask of dust; and each would dig his slit trench. By half-past eight, all would be asleep except for the sentries.

From Bernard Fergusson, *The Black Watch and the King's Enemies*, Collins, 1950.

Questions

1 In what way does Fergusson's account confirm information on the map?

2 If you had followed this routine for two months, what would have been your main memory?

3 Why do you think the Allies landed in Morocco and Algeria in November 1943?

4 What does the map suggest about the importance of the battle of El Alamein?

5 Imagine a German soldier's account of the same time in the desert. What might he write about?

25 At Monte Cassino 1943

After the Germans had been driven out of North Africa the Allies landed in Sicily and thrust towards Italy and Rome. The Italians surrendered, but German forces in Italy were strengthened, so the Allies had to fight their way north over the Apennine mountains south of Rome. The German line hinged round the monastery at Cassino which dominated the road north. The monastery was destroyed by bombs in February 1944. It has been rebuilt today. The extract is taken from an account by a soldier, Fred Majdalany, of the build up of the final attack on Cassino.

A Portrait of a battle

From then on the din was continuous and simultaneous: the thunder of the guns, the hugely amplified staccato of the shell-burst close in front, and the vicious overhead scream that linked them with a frenzied counterpoint. And sometimes the scream became a whinny, and sometimes a kind of red-hot angry baleful scream. The fury of it was elemental, yet precise. It was a controlled cyclone. It was splendid to hear, as the moment of actual combat approached.

The makers of films like to represent this scene with shots of soldiers crouching dramatically in readiness, and close-ups of tense, grim faces. Whereas the striking thing about such moments is the matter-of-factness and casualness of the average soldier. It is true that hearts are apt to be thumping fairly hard, and everyone is thinking, 'Oh, Christ!' But you don't in fact look grim and intense. For one thing you would look slightly foolish if you did. For another you have too many things to do.

The two leading companies were due to advance exactly eight minutes after the barrage opened. So those eight minutes were spent doing such ordinary things as tying up boot laces, helping each other with their equipment, urinating, giving weapons a final check, testing wireless sets to make certain they were still netted, eating a bar of chocolate. The officers were giving last-minute instructions, marshalling their men into battle formations, or having a final check-up with the tank commanders with whom they were going to work.

Those who were not in the leading companies were digging like fiends, for they knew that the temporary calm would be quickly shattered as soon as the tanks and the leading infantry were seen emerging from it.

Meanwhile the barrage thundered on, and to its noise was added the roar of the Shermans' engines. A great bank of dust and smoke welled slowly up from the area the shells were pounding, so that you couldn't see the bursts any more. The sputtering of the 25-pounders

From Fred Majdalany, *The Monastery*, Bodley Head, 1945.

rippled up and down the breadth of the gun-lines faster than bullets from a machine-gun, so numerous were they.

At eight minutes past nine they moved. Geoff led his company round the right end, Mark led his round the left end of the bank which concealed us from the enemy in front. Then the Shermans clattered forward, with a crescendo of engine-roar that made even shouted conversation impossible. The battle was on.

Questions

1 What was it about the bombardment which made Fred Majdalany think it was 'splendid to hear'?

2 What does the writer suggest is wrong about the way film-makers show soldiers just before a screen 'battle'?

3 Use the account to explain how tanks and infantry worked together in this battle.

4 Imagine you were a tank commander in this battle. Write your account of the scene as the battle began.

5 Suggest why the British army commander thought that Cassino must be captured.

26 Pacific war 1

By the summer of 1942 the Japanese controlled all South-east Asia and the West Pacific and had built a war-time empire or 'co-prosperity sphere'. The only challenge to their power in the area now came from the US navy. On 4 June 1942 the Battle of Midway was fought between carrier forces of the two navies. The Japanese were full of their success after Pearl Harbour (see page 42) and their fleet of 4 carriers and about 270 aircraft engaged 3 American carriers with their 240 aircraft. The battle was fought between two fleets over 160 kilometres apart. The Japanese were defeated and the Americans could begin a counter-attack on the well-defended Japanese positions. The extract is taken from A Record of the War published in 1943.

A Pacific War: the Japanese
The Japanese co-prosperity sphere

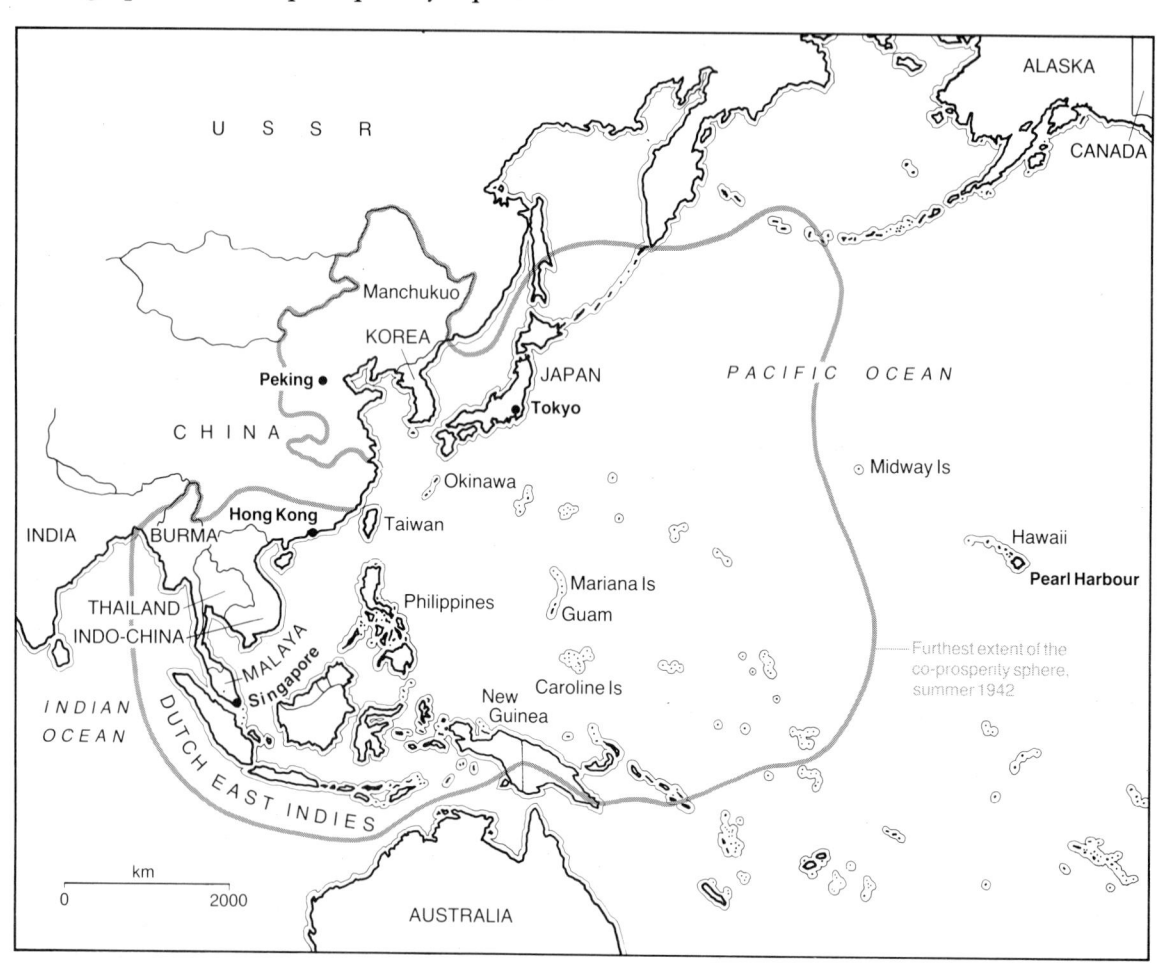

B The Battle of Midway 1942

During the attack on the *Yorktown* some of her own aircraft found the *Hiryu* in the company of battleships, cruisers and destroyers. They left the *Hiryu* blazing from stem to stern. Two battleships and a heavy cruiser were badly hit and a destroyer was believed to have been sunk. That afternoon an American submarine scored three hits on the aircraft carrier *Soryu*. At sunset heavy explosions and billows of smoke arose from her hull. She sank during the night. Just before sunset on 4 June US Army bombers attacked several burning or crippled ships. They scored three hits on an aircraft carrier, believed to be the *Akagi*, set a cruiser on fire and claimed a destroyer as sunk. By now four Japanese aircraft carriers were out of action. The *Akagi* was not seen again. The *Soryu* was sinking in flames. The *Hiryu* sank early in the morning of 5 June.

From *A Record of the War: The Eleventh Quarter, April 1 1942-June 30 1942*, Hutchinson, 1943.

Questions

1 Compare Map A and Map B on page 41. What does Map A tell you about Japanese successes since 1940?

2 Use the maps to suggest what problems the Japanese government would have in controlling and defending their 1942 empire.

3 Find Midway Island and Hawaii (Pearl Harbour) on the map. How far is Midway from Hawaii and from Japan?

4 Why was control of the sea and air so important in this area?

5 What was the job of the battleships, cruisers and destroyers in this battle?

6 What else did the Japanese lose when their carriers were sunk?

7 Imagine you were an American pilot at Midway. Write a letter home describing the battle.

27 Pacific war 2

Much of the land in the co-prosperity sphere was jungle, and the Japanese had learned how to move swiftly through it as they fought to the death to keep the lands they had conquered. Many Allied soldiers fighting this determined enemy in terrible conditions felt neglected by people at home and called themselves 'the Forgotten Army'. The first extract is from Jungle is Neutral *by Spencer Chapman, 1949, and describes the Japanese advancing on Singapore through Malaya in 1942 and the British troops facing them. The second extract is an account by an American engineer who fought in New Guinea, published in 1956. Source C is taken from the Order issued by the Japanese Major-General Tanaka to his thirty-third Division in Burma.*

A Two armies in Malaya

The majority were on bicycles in parties of forty or fifty, riding three or four abreast and talking and laughing just as if they were going to a football match. Indeed, some of them were actually wearing football jerseys; they seemed to have no standard uniform or equipment and were travelling as light as they possibly could.

Our front-line soldiers were at this time equipped like Christmas trees with heavy boots, web equipment, packs, harepacks, water bottles, blankets, ground sheets and even greatcoats and respirators, so that they could hardly walk much less fight.

From F. Spencer Chapman, *Jungle is Neutral*, Chatto and Windus, 1949.

B New Guinea

The problems of climate and health were no less severe. The penetrating, energy-sapping heat was accompanied by intense humidity and frequent torrential rains that defy description. Health conditions were amongst the worst in the world. The incidence of malaria could only be reduced by the most rigid and irksome discipline and even then the dreaded disease took a heavy toll. . . . Scrub typhus, ringworm, hookworm and yaws all awaited the careless soldier. Millions of insects clouded everywhere. Clouds of mosquitoes, flies, leeches, chiggers, ants, fleas and other parasites pestered man night and day. Disease was an unrelenting foe.

From C. Willoughby and J. Chamberlain, *MacArthur, 1941–1957: Victory in the Pacific*, Heinemann, 1956.

C A General's Order

... it must be expected that the division will be almost annihilated. I have confidence in your firm courage and devotion and believe that you will do your duty, but should any delinquencies occur you have got to understand that I shall take the necessary action ...

From Viscount Slim, *Defeat into victory*, Cassell, 1956.

Questions

1 From Spencer Chapman's account which army was most prepared for jungle warfare?

2 Use Source B to describe the problems of an army commander preparing for a jungle campaign.

3 What two reasons are suggested by General Tanaka's Order for the brave and fierce fighting by the Japanese?

28 Germany Bombed

In 1940 the Luftwaffe changed from bombing airfields which were difficult to hit and destroy, to the 'blitz' on cities. The British followed the same policy with 'area' bombing of German cities, which grew heavier in each year of its use. Source A is from Churchill's cabinet memorandum of 3 September 1940 which explains some of the aims of the bombing. Pilots found it difficult to fly through German defences, as Diagram B shows, and almost impossible to pin-point and hit a single factory or railway station. German war-time production reached its peak in March 1944, just when Allied bombing was at its heaviest. The extract in C is taken from My Childhood in Nazi Germany *by Ilse Koehn, published 1977. Ilse had gone out to collect the milk one day when a bomber raid took place.*

A Churchill's memorandum

The Navy can lose us the war, but only the Air Force can win it. Therefore our supreme effort must be to gain overwhelming mastery in the air. The Fighters are our salvation, but the Bombers alone provide the means of victory. We must, therefore, develop the power to carry an ever-increasing number of explosives to Germany, so as to pulverize the entire industry and scientific structure on which the war effort and economic life of the enemy depend.

From N. R. Bomford, *World History 1914–70*, Edward Arnold, 1973.

B The German defence system

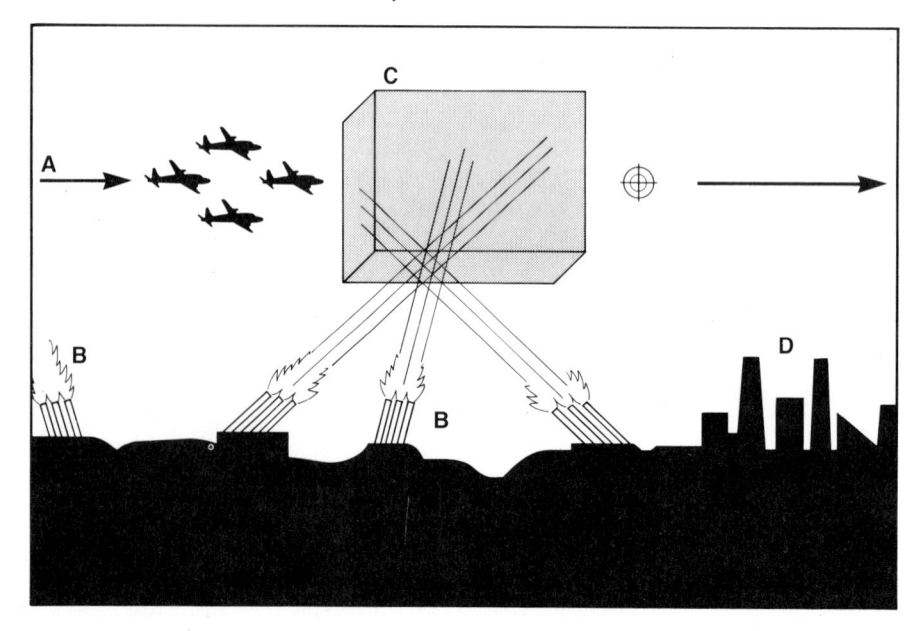

A	Flight path of attacking bombers
B	Anti-aircraft gun batteries
C	Box through which bombers had to pass
D	Target area
⊕	Bomb release point

C A bomber raid

Oh, my God! What a sight! Hundreds, thousands of airplanes are coming toward us! The whole sky is aglitter with planes. Planes flying undisturbed in perfect V formation their metal bodies sparkling in the sun. And no anti-aircraft guns. Only the terrifying, quickly intensifying hum of engines, thousands of engines. The air vibrates, seems to shiver; the water, the ground and the bridge under us begin to tremble. It's unearthly, a tremendously beautiful sight! A whole blue sky full of silver planes.

We run. The first formation is already overhead. All hell breaks loose. The anti-aircraft guns shoot and bombs fall like rain. Millions of long-rounded shapes come tumbling down around us. The sky turns grey, black, the earth erupts. The detonations begin to sound like continuous thunder.

A house! Shelter from this nightmare. We reach it, though I don't know how. I collide with the old lady who is standing in the door. She tries to take the baby away from me. We stand in the doorway entangled by the pail, and I see the bomb, watch it hit the roof, and see the house cave in behind her.

'God in heaven!' she screams. 'God in heaven!'

'Grandma! Grandma!' wails the little girl, pulling at her skirt.

'Grandma, let's go to the bunker, please, please, Grandma!'

I'm flat on the ground. Bombs, bombs, bombs fall all around me. It can't be. It's a dream. There aren't that many bombs in the whole world. Maybe I'm dead? I get up, drag pail, old woman and girl with me toward a porch, a concrete porch with space underneath. Above the detonations, flak fire, shattering glass rises the old woman's high-pitched voice: 'God in heaven! God in Heaven!' And now the baby is wailing too.

From Ilse Koehn, *Mischling, Second Degree*, Greenwillow Books, Bantam, 1977.

Questions

1 What was happening when Churchill wrote his memorandum?

2 Explain why fighters meant 'salvation' but the bombers 'victory'.

3 What does Churchill give as the main aim of the bombing raids? Does Source C suggest another result?

4 What difficulties can you find from the diagram to carrying out the plan?

5 Why do you think pin-point bombing did not work?

6 What evidence is there in Ilse's account that the main effect of the bombing was to terrorise the civilians in Germany?

29 The Allies work together

In January 1943 Roosevelt and Churchill met at Casablanca in North Africa. Stalin was invited, but said he was unable to leave the USSR as he was commander in chief of the Soviet armies. Roosevelt and Churchill announced that the objective of the war was to get the unconditional surrender of Germany, Italy and Japan. In December 1943 Roosevelt, Churchill and Stalin met at Teheran. There the Russians were informed of Anglo-American plans for the opening of a second-front by 'Overlord' – a cross-channel invasion of France in the summer of 1944. The first extract is taken from the official report from Casablanca and the second from Churchill's Second World War, *describing decisions made at Teheran and his anxiety that Stalin had a true picture of the British attitude.*

A Communiqué from Casablanca

The entire field of the war was surveyed, theater by theater, throughout the world, and all resources were marshalled for a more intense prosecution of the war by sea, land and air.

Nothing like this prolonged discussion between two Allies has ever taken place before. Complete agreement was reached between the leaders of the two countries and their respective staffs upon the war plans and enterprises to be undertaken during the campaigns of 1943 against Germany, Italy and Japan, with a view to drawing the utmost advantage from the markedly favorable turn of events at the close of 1942.

From L. L. Snyder, Fifty Major Documents of the Twentieth Century, Anvil Books, Van Nostrand, 1955.

B Operation 'Overlord'

Now about 'Overlord'. The British would have ready by the date fixed in May or June nearly sixteen divisions, with their corps troops, landing-craft troops, anti-aircraft, and services, a total of slightly over half a million men. These would consist of some of our best troops, including battle-trained men from the Mediterranean. In addition the British would have all that was needed from the Royal Navy to handle transportation and to protect the Army, and there would be the metropolitan Air Forces of about 4000 first-line British aircraft in continuous action. The American import of troops was now beginning. Up till now they had sent mainly air troops and stores for the Army, but in the next four or five months I thought 150,000 men or more would come every month, making a total of seven to eight hundred thousand men by May. The defeat of the submarines in the Atlantic

From W. S. Churchill, Second World War Vol. 5, Cassell, 1952.

had made this movement possible. I was in favour of launching the operation in the South of France about the same time as 'Overlord' or at whatever moment was found correct. We should be holding enemy troops in Italy, and of the twenty-two or twenty-three divisions in the Mediterranean as many as possible would go to the South of France and the rest would remain in Italy. . . .

Stalin said he must warn me that the Red Army was depending on the success of our invasion of Northern France. If there were no operations in May 1944 then the Red Army would think that there would be no operations at all that year. The weather would be bad and there would be transport difficulties. If the operation did not take place he did not want the Red Army to be disappointed. Disappointment could only create bad feeling. If there was no big change in the European war in 1944 it would be very difficult for the Russians to carry on. They were war-weary. He feared that a feeling of isolation might develop in the Red Army.

Questions

1 From Source A do you think that the agreement upon 'unconditional surrender' at Casablanca was important?

2 What does extract A tell you about the mood of the Allies early in 1943?

3 Why was Stalin unable to leave Moscow in January 1943?

4 Why did Stalin warn Churchill that 'Overlord' must take place on time?

5 Were Roosevelt, Stalin and Churchill really close in alliance or are there signs of differences of purpose in Churchill's account?

6 What is the value of a statesman's account of events in which he played an important part?

Part 6

Partisans, prisoners and war production

30 Partisans 1

By 1942 the Germans had conquered most of Europe. Throughout occupied Europe the Gestapo, the Nazi secret police, maintained a reign of terror. Against this the partisans fought as well as they could, and the Allies attempted to keep these flickering flames of resistance alive. The picture shows German soldiers hanging Russian partisans. The extract is taken from Uncle Misha's Partisans *by Yuri Suhl published in 1975. It is a fictional account based on the actual experiences of a group of Ukrainian Jewish partisans in the Ukraine, which is in the western USSR and which was occupied by the Nazis.*

A Public execution in Minsk, October 1941

B The partisan band

Once, not so long ago, they remembered, they too had enjoyed the warmth of home and the love of family. Now their homes were gone. Total strangers sat at the tables they had sat at, slept in the beds they had slept in, wore the clothes they had worn. And their families – fathers, mothers, wives, children – were all heaped in some unmarked mass grave, together with cherished dreams and cherished hopes, a bulging mound of earth the only monument to their unlived lives.

And they, the 'lucky' ones, who by some miracle had managed to escape the executioner's bullet, had vowed to avenge them and destroy the destroyer of human life. Their home was the forest; the open sky their roof; their fellow partisans the only family they had; their most precious possession, their weapons. Each night, under cover of darkness, they would emerge from the forest in twos, in threes, in tens, and fan out in various directions, a silent invisible army of Jewish fighters in search of the enemy.

From Yuri Suhl, *Uncle Misha's Partisans*, Hamish Hamilton, 1975.

Questions

1. In what way does the picture help to explain the fact that so many people fought for the partisans in occupied Europe?

2. What does the novelist give as the reasons for the determination of the partisans?

3. Does Source B suggest ways in which a story based on an actual incident can have advantages and disadvantages as historical evidence compared with an account from the event itself?

4. Discuss the reasons for people accepting Nazi occupation or for joining the partisans.

31 Partisans 2

The French partisans were organised into sabotage groups, or maquis. George Miller was a member of the maquis and in Source A he describes how a partisan, Phillipe, helped with the wrecking of two trains. The extract is taken from George Miller's book Maquis, *published in 1945. Source B describes how a Norwegian agent, Oluf Reed Olsen, arrived back in Norway. It is taken from his book* Two Eggs on my Plate, *published in 1952.*

A Sabotage on the railways

Unable to avoid the scene of his crime, he cycled past the still smoking remains where the Gestapo were examining tracks and questioning civilians and railwaymen. He saw another locomotive in Miserey station. Unarmed as he was, he cursed and swore at the railwaymen until they sent their engine rushing down the track. It hit the wreckage while the Gestapo were still there, and jumping, said onlookers, thirty feet [9 metres] into the air it landed upside down on the other side of the heap of twisted metal. Its wheels continued to revolve for some time. Already crowds were gathering for this fantastic sight. Cycling excursions were setting out from all the villages. Many of them were to have their money's worth. Philippe, tranquilly continuing on his way to Besançon, found another train and again, with only his gruff and determined voice to help him succeeded in getting it launched at full speed on the right rails. In front of a large audience this train added itself to the heap in the cutting.

From George Miller, *Maquis*, Heinemann, 1945.

B Night landing

I just collapsed at the foot of the fir-tree like a pile of wet rags and lay there with closed eyes. I stretched out my hand, caught hold of a piece of reindeer moss, and inhaled its scent. Never, never, would anyone make me do another parachute jump; indeed, I never wanted to see a plane again!

This was Norway: Norwegian fir and pine, Norwegian bilberry and reindeer moss. Despite the burning pain in my back and knee I could not help enjoying their familiar scent, taking long draughts of the night air.

From Oluf Reed Olsen, *Two Eggs on my Plate*, Allen and Unwin, 1952.

Questions

1 Imagine you were one of the spectators who cycles to the scene described in Source A. What account will you give of the day's events?

2 Imagine you were one of the railwaymen at Miserey or Besançon. What would go through your mind as you decided to send the trains?

3 Does the passage give any clues about why the Germans found the maquis difficult to check?

4 What does Source B tell you about the difficulty of getting agents into occupied Europe?

5 Why do you think Olsen could not help enjoying the night air?

32 Prisoners

The Japanese controlled the lowlands of China and nearly all the countries and islands of South East Asia by 1942 (see map on page 52). They wanted to link Burma and Thailand without having to use the sea route, so decided to build a railway across 850 kilometres of mountains and monsoon jungle. For labour they used European and American prisoners of war. Every 25 metres of track claimed one victim as half-starved men worked in one of the most unhealthy climates in the world. Dr Robert Hardie, a medical officer in Malaya, was taken prisoner by the Japanese after the fall of Singapore. He was a prisoner for three years and kept a diary which he managed to conceal from the Japanese. This diary was published by the Imperial War Museum in 1983. Source A is from the section headed 5 May 1943, and describes a transit camp. The second extract shows the terrible boredom for prisoners of war in Germany. The account is from Goon in the Black *by Eric Williams, an air force officer who was in several prisoner-of-war camps.*

A The secret diary

We slept crammed in our tents on the damp ground. At Colonel Johnson's request I took over medical supervision of the officer's battalion and the more thankless job of arguing with the Japanese in charge of our party about the disposal of sick men who were unable to keep on with the march. The track on which we were travelling was just adequate for vehicles so that if we did have to leave men behind they could be brought on by lorry. At this camp we did not have to ask for any such assistance however. Next morning we started again shortly after dawn, thus making use of the cool part of the day. It was a short march again, ending about midday, this time in a wide natural clearing surrounded by rocky jungle-covered hills. A considerable number of rather dilapidated tents – roofs only, no sides – were already pitched here, and these we occupied. Food was provided for us by a party from one of the Kanuy camps about a mile away. Rogers, once of Bukit Jalil estate near Kuala Lumpur, was among these cooks. A stream which crossed the track about a quarter of a mile beyond the clearing was our water supply, and below the water drawing point one was able to get a wash. A Japanese notice here, addressed to 'Coolies and Prisoners of War', delimited the water-drawing and the washing zones.

From Robert Hardie, *The Burma-Siam Railway*, Imperial War Museum, 1983.

B Boredom in Germany

It was lunch time. The biscuits had not been buttered. No one had gone for the tea water. Five morose figures sat round a naked table. Presently Pomfret spoke. 'It's a matter of principle. I've done it every day this week and now it's Friday. It's not that I mind doing it, but I've done more than my share. Clinton must do it to-day as a matter of principle.' He advanced his chin obstinately. He was dressed in the full uniform of a flight-lieutenant. His collar, ironed with a tin of hot water, was frayed round the edges.

'That's all very well,' said Bennett, 'but it's lunch time and we're hungry. You and Clinton share the duty of cook and it's up to you to see that the meal is prepared.' Bennett, apart from his odd assortment of clothes, might have been addressing a board meeting. He delivered his opinion as an ultimatum and glanced round the table for approval. His red, hairy arms were crossed upon the table. Having delivered his speech, he sucked his teeth with an air of finality.

From Eric Williams, *The Goon in Black*, Jonathan Cape, 1945.

Questions

1 Why did Dr Hardie describe his arguments with the Japanese as 'thankless'?

2 How might Dr Hardie have known the camp cook before the war?

3 What do you learn about Japanese attitudes to prisoners of war from this extract?

4 Why were the water-drawing and washing zones 'delimited'?

5 Why were the figures round the table 'morose'?

6 Suggest what the behaviour and dress of these men tell you about the effects of prison life.

33 The final solution

The Jews suffered most in Hitler's Europe. In January 1942 Reinhard Heydrich, commander of the Gestapo, called a conference at Wannsee to discuss the 'final solution'. Source A is from the Wannsee Protocol which set out the agreed arrangement. The largest number of Jewish victims came from Poland where, out of a Jewish population of 3,300,000, 2,800,000 were killed. Source B is from The Survivor *by Jack Eisner, 1980. Jack Eisner won a scholarship to the Warsaw Music Conservatory in 1939 when he was thirteen. Instead of studying music he became an inhabitant of the Jewish ghetto in Warsaw. Half a million Jews died in Warsaw, but Jack Eisner survived to tell his story. He now lives and works in New York. His account is of an incident during his journey with Jewish prisoners from Warsaw to the Treblinka death camp. The barracks were said to have showers for disinfecting the prisoners but Eisner knew they were gas chambers when he saw the sealed windows.*

A The Wannsee Protocol

The final solution to the Jewish problem in Europe will be applied to about eleven million people.... The Jews must be transferred to the East under close surveillance and there assigned to forced labour.... It goes without saying that a great many of them will be naturally eliminated by physical deficiency. The remainder who survive this – and who must be regarded as the most resistant group – must be dealt with accordingly. Indeed, history has shown us that this natural elite carries within itself the seeds of a new Jewish renaissance....

From S. Friedländer, in *History of the Twentieth Century*, Purnell, 1969.

B Jewish prisoners

My eyes followed the line. The woman and her newly adopted child were now only moments away from the decision of life or death. They climbed the wooden barracks steps. The SS doctor pulled away the raincoat. Silence for a moment, as he sized up the child and the woman.

'She can walk. Can't she?'

The woman nodded.

'Put her down then. Los!'

An SS aide stepped forward and pulled the girl from the woman.

'Here. Here's where you go.' The white-clad SS officer pointed to the barracks entrance only a few feet away.

The little girl began to cry loudly and sat down.

'You can either go with her or not,' the SS officer barked at the woman. 'But schnell. Make up your mind.'

In an instant, the sadistic bastard had transferred the choice of life or death from himself to the woman. She could abandon the child and save herself, or she could accompany the child.

From Jack Eisner, *The Survivor*, Sphere Books, 1982.

The woman's conflict was so apparent, it was heartbreaking. She moved slowly toward the girl, and death; then quickly away to the left, for life. She hesitated, then once again walked back to the girl. Her hair was in wild disarray. Her mouth was clenched. Her conscience was tearing her apart.

The SS doctor quickly tired of his sport. He ordered his aide to shove both the woman and the child into the barracks. The storm trooper grabbed the hesitating woman's arm and pushed her forward. She fell over the little girl's body.

'Move. Los!'

Suddenly a screaming young woman ran wildly up the steps. It was the child's real mother. She pushed the storm trooper aside and threw herself on the crying little girl. She kissed her face, arm and head. She comforted her. She covered the child's body with her own.

Even the SS men stared in wonder for a moment. But not for long. In violent reaction, the storm trooper she had pushed levelled his machine gun and pulled the trigger, bringing the entire episode to an abrupt end. The mother, the child and the middle-aged woman were grotesquely sprawled in their own blood only a few feet from the barracks entrance.

How efficient those Germans are, I thought. They create a dilemma. And they solve it. Decisively.

Questions

1 What did Heydrich mean in Source A by stating that many Jews would be 'eliminated by physical deficiency'?

2 Why did he argue that the strongest group must be destroyed?

3 What did he feel that history had shown from earlier persecutions of the Jews?

4 How did the SS officer in Source B transfer the choice of life or death to the woman?

5 Why did the SS men stare in wonder for a moment?

6 Do these extracts explain the meaning of the term 'the final solution'?

34 British women at war

The strain of fighting a modern war was felt by everybody. Governments made war industries a priority. The first picture shows Churchill visiting an aeroplane factory in Birmingham where he is watching a girl rivetter at work on a Spitfire. Source B is from O Dreams, O Destinations *by the writer Phyllis Bentley, published in 1962. She sums up the vital part played by women at home. The final pictures show members of the Women's Auxiliary Airforce, WAAF, on the march in 1940 and 'lumberjills' of the Women's Land Army.*

A

B   Fighting the war at home

... living the ordinary life of the middle-aged provincial woman of the day, taught me how right Ernest Bevin was when he remarked later that the women tipped the scales of victory. It was not only that seven million women in the armed forces, civil defence, agriculture and industry, packed the parachutes, typed the forms, drove the tractors and milked the cows, filled the shells, waterproofed the tanks assembled the radio sets, kept the transport running, put out the incendiary bombs, worked the trip hammers.... But it was the ordinary housewife who was in fact decisive. She could have lost the war in any one week. Struggling to feed and clothe her family amid rations and coupons – meat and milk and butter and cheese and margarine and tea and sugar and eggs and soap were rationed, clothes and sweets could only be bought by coupons – if she had once revolted... the whole system would have become unworkable.

Phyllis Bentley, *O Dreams, O Destinations*, Gollancz, 1962.

C Women at war

Newly recruited WAAFs watch well-trained girls march by.

Members of the Womens Timber Corps training at Bury St Edmunds, January 1943.

Questions

1 Why do you think the prime minister was photographed in this way?

2 What does Phyllis Bentley say about her life during the war to support the conclusion she comes to in Source B?

3 How does Source B suggest the ordinary housewife could have lost the war in a week?

4 Suggest ways of summarising the list of civilian jobs described by Phyllis Bentley.

5 Write a short piece for a local paper on Britain's unsung heroines.

6 What do the pictures show about the part played by women in the war?

7 Suggest ways in which war work led to changes in the post-war position of women in society.

35 Scientists go to war

Fighting men in all armies were aware of the work of 'boffins', the scientists and technologists working on new ways of attack and defence. Many of these developments, such as radar, the rocket and the atomic bomb, were based on scientific discoveries made before the war. Source A is from The First and the Last *by the German air commander, Colonel Adolf Galland, published in 1955. He describes his first sight of the plane and then his feelings as he flew. In Source B from* Follow my Leader, *1951, Louis Hagen quotes a German storm trooper who pinned all his hopes in 1944 on science and technology. He mentions the V1 rockets which did great damage in Britain in late 1944 and 1945. The picture C is of one of Major-General Hobart's 'funnies'. A Sherman tank has been modified so that it can cut a path through minefields.*

A Flying without propellors

I shall never forget 22 May 1943, the day I flew a jet aircraft for the first time in my life. In the early morning I met Messerschmitt on his testing airfield, Lechfeld, near the main works at Augsburg.

... We drove out to the runway. There stood the two Me.262 jet-fighters, the reason for our meeting and for all our great hopes. An unusual sight, these planes without airscrews. Covered by a streamlined cowling, two nacelles under the wings housed the jet engines. None of the engineers could tell us how many horse-power they developed.

.... The flying speed of 520 mph [840 kph] in horizontal flights, which was fantastic at that time, meant an advance of at least 120 mph [200 kph] over the fastest propeller-driven aircraft. Inferior fuel similar to diesel oil could be used instead of octane, which was more and more difficult to get.

.... For the first time I was flying by jet propulsion! No engine vibration, no torque, and no lashing noise from the air-screw. Accompanied by a whistling sound, my jet shot through the air. Later, when asked what it felt like, I said, 'It was as though angels were pushing'.

From Adolf Galland, *The First and the Last*, Methuen 1955.

B Faith in the Führer

There was a lot of talk about the wonder weapons. We learned that our scientists had developed entirely new types of planes with four to five times the present speed, and these were now ready waiting for the Führer to give the order to go into action. And the real 'wonder' weapons had shown during their trials that their power of destruction was so immense that anything we had developed before was a joke in comparison. That was why we were almost crazy with joy when we heard that the first secret weapon, the V1, was at last being used against Britain. There was panic in London, the town was in flames, and we saw again how the Führer had kept his word.

From Louis Hagan, *Follow My Leader*, Allan Wingate, 1951.

C Sherman flail tank

Questions

1 Why were the two planes described in Source A an unusual sight at the time?

2 List the advantages that Galland states these jets had over propellor driven 'planes'.

3 What was the main difference Galland noticed when he flew?

4 What was the secret weapon, the VI?

5 Does the storm trooper's memory (B) tell most about the new weapons or the state of mind of German soldiers in 1944?

6 Existing tanks were made into 'funnies'. Why was this a serious business?

Part 7

The ring closes 1944–5

36 D-Day

The second front was opened in 1944 by the landings in Normandy on 6 June 1944. The build-up in England had been careful and secret and the Germans were taken by surprise but fought the landings bitterly. Source A is taken from the official history of the Argyll and Sutherland Highlanders, Fifth Battalion, by Major Desmond Flower, published in 1950. Source B gives the recollections of Madame Bernadette Renouf of the seaside town of Arromanches. She was twenty-two at the time of the D-Day landings. Her account was collected by Philip Warner for his book The D-Day Landings *(1980).*

A Gathering forces

Our destination was Southampton, eighty-seven miles [140 km] away by direct route, but well over a hundred by the way we were required to take to conform with the traffic arrangements which spread like a cat's cradle over the whole of southern England.

... by three o'clock in the afternoon we had got to the marshalling area on Southampton Common, the drivers remaining with their vehicles while the remainder were firmly imprisoned within barbed wire. Everyone who had been in the main column was suffering from eye strain, varying from a minimum slight soreness to Lieutenant Pothecary, who lost his sight completely and for some time had to be led about. This disturbing and painful ailment was brought about partly by the dust, and partly by the diesel fumes thrown up by M.10s travelling head to tail, for the roads approaching all South Coast ports carried so much traffic that normal road discipline was abandoned and the order was 'close up and get on'.

From D. Flower, *History of the Argyll and Sutherland Highlanders, 5th Battalion, 91st Anti-Tank Regiment, 1939–45*, Thomas Nelson, 1950.

B A young woman in Normandy

I must say here that all that section of the road where we were was houses, and part had been evacuated in October 1943 and some of the houses had been actually taken over by the Germans, and one on the corner of the Rue de la Marine was occupied by officers. I don't know what rank, and also there were troops there. And we saw them running, one losing his boots, losing their caps, trying to get on bicycles, fixing their things on their backs, and – oh, it was lovely! Then I remember I said something which was not very distinguished in a young woman – but I said it.

Then we called Papa and told him and he said we must all get dressed because something was certainly going to happen. Then sometime towards morning, I'm not sure of the exact time but when it had started to get light, my brother was called by a neighbour of ours, a Monsieur Georges Aligot. He slept on the second floor of a house just opposite ours. He said, 'Come and see'. Naturally, without thinking, because we weren't supposed to go outside before 6 o'clock, we rushed across to look. And then, in front of the Hotel de Normandie, we had a view on to the sea, and it was really something.

It was splendid with the sun just coming up, we could see a multitude of ships, but a multitude.... What we felt is almost indescribable, we were suffocated by emotion. Just suffocated. I have a son, and I have tried to tell him what I felt at that moment, but it just isn't possible to convey it. I can only say suffocated by the sight. No one can imagine how tremendous it was, what a splendid spectacle.

From Philip Warner, *The D-Day Landings*, William Kimber, 1980.

Questions

1. Why did the traffic arrangements spread like a cat's cradle over Southern England?
2. Why were the troops placed within barbed wire?
3. What happened to the drivers and why?
4. What was 'so lovely' about the sight Madame Renouf saw on 6 June?
5. What clues are there in Source B to show that it is a piece of 'oral history'?
6. Why does she find it so difficult to tell her son about the landings?
7. Imagine you were a German soldier in Arromanches that morning. Describe your feelings.

37 Advance into Germany

In 1944 and early 1945 the Germans were caught in a closing ring, with the Americans and British advancing into Germany from the west and the Red Army from the east. Source A is from a novel, The Young Lions, *by Irwin Shaw published in 1949. Irwin Shaw was in the American army and fought in the West. He writes about Noah and Rickett, two soldiers in the army advancing through France and into Germany. Source B is from* The Only Way Out *by R. M. Wingfield, published in 1955. Wingfield was a British soldier who fought with the advancing allied armies and wrote an account of the fighting. The third extract is from* Russia at War 1941–1945 *by Alexander Werth, 1964. He is telling the story of a nineteen-year-old boy, Mitya Khludov, whose family lived in Moscow and knew Werth. Mitya was in an artillery unit and wrote this letter to Werth in 1944. He died in a military hospital not long after. His letter mentions Ilya Ehrenburg, who was another Russian journalist.*

A Shooting a tank

Noah braced himself rigidly against the window frame. He was sure that he was going to be shot in a moment. His entire body from the waist up was fully exposed in the window. He stared down at the waving guns of the tank, obscure in the growing shadows of dusk in the lane.

Then Rickett fired. The bazooka shell moved very deliberately through the air. Then it exploded against the tank. Noah watched from the window, forgetting to get down. Nothing seemed to happen for a moment. Then the cannon swung heavily downwards, stopped, pointing at the ground. There was an explosion inside the tank, muffled and deep. Some wisps of smoke came up through the driver's slits and the edges of the hatch. Then there were many more explosions. The tank rocked and quivered where it stood. Then the explosions stopped. The tank still looked as dangerous and full of malice as before, but it did not move. Noah saw the infantrymen behind it running. They ran down the lane, with no one firing at them, and disappeared behind the edge of the shed.

'It works, ah reckon,' Rickett said. 'Ah think we have shot ourselves a tank.' He took the bazooka off Noah's shoulder and put it against the wall.

From Irwin Shaw, *The Young Lions*, World Books Edition, 1949.

B The Western advance

We felt quite a professional affection for these paratroops. They were infantry trained, like us, to use their own initiative. They had the same system of 'trench-mates'. They fought cleanly and treated prisoners, wounded and dead, with the same respect they expected from us. If our uniforms had been the same, we would have welcomed them as kindred spirits.

From R. M. Wingfield, *The Only Way Out*, Hutchinson, 1955.

On one occasion the paratroops acquitted themselves as the honourable gentlemen we later knew them to be. It was the first time many of us had ever seen them. We never forgot them.

We had attacked a wood and been thrown out. The platoon was being 'stonked' in a ditch. Two of our stretcher bearers went out to collect a casualty hit in the leg by a splinter. As soon as the Medics appeared, small-arms fire stopped as if turned off at the main. Unfortunately the German mortars could not see the target and sent over one more bomb before the 'cease-fire' reached them. That bomb hit one of the stretcher-bearers in the leg. One stretcher-bearer was left in No Man's Land with two casualties and one stretcher.

Immediately two German paras burst out of the woods, holding up their hands to show that they were not armed. They ran to the group in the field. They loaded the two casualties on to the stretcher in sitting positions, and, under the direction of the surviving Medic, they carried the men to safety in our lines. Waving farewell, they doubled back to the wood. We cheered them all the way back. A twelve-hour truce followed. No one had the heart to spoil this gesture by firing. So, temporarily, the war stopped. Next morning they had gone.

C The Soviet advance

I am proud to be in the Party, to be one of Stalin's victorious soldiers. If I'm lucky enough I'll be in Berlin yet. We'll get there – and we deserve to get there – before our Western Allies do. If you see Ehrenburg, give him my regards. Tell him we all have been reading his stuff .... Tell him we really hate the Germans after seeing so many horrors they have committed here in Belorussia. Not to mention all the destruction they've caused. They've pretty well turned this country into a desert.

From A. Werth, *Russia at War 1941–45*, Barrie Books, 1964.

Questions

1. What does the end of the German tank in Source A show you about the kind of fighting in France?

2. What sort of weapon was a bazooka?

3. In Source B what examples does the writer give to support his view that the German paratroops were the same kind of people as the British infantry?

4. Why did Mitya hate the Germans?

5. Contrast Winfield's extract with Mitya's letter to Alexander Werth. What evidence is there of different attitudes to the Germans?

6. Why should Mitya believe the Red Army deserved to be first in Berlin?

38 Germany in despair

In March 1945 the Allied armies in the west crossed the Rhine, while in the east Vienna fell to the advancing Russians on 13 April. The Germans feared the avenging Red Army from the east most of all. From the underground bunker headquarters in Berlin Hitler issued his last order on 16 April, and part of it is printed as Source A. Source B is taken from Else Wendel's Hausfrau at War, *published 1957. She describes soldiers in Berlin facing the Russian advance. They had been promised reinforcements led by General Wenk.*

A Hitler's last order

He who at this moment does not do his duty is a traitor to the German nation. The regiments or divisions that relinquish their posts are acting so disgracefully that they must hang their heads in shame before the women and children who here in our cities are braving the terror bombing.

. . . If during these next days and weeks every soldier in the east does his duty, Asia's final onslaught will come to nought – just as the invasion of our Western enemies will in the end fail.

Berlin stays German. Vienna will be German again. And Europe will never be Russian!

Rise up to defend your homes, your women, your children – rise up to defend your own future!

At this hour the eyes of the German nation are upon you, you, my fighters in the east, hoping that your steadfastness, your ardour, and your arms will smother the Bolshevist attack in a sea of blood!

From J. Thorwald, *Flight in the Winter*, Hutchinson, 1953.

B Fighting to the last boy

To my astonishment one of the soldiers burst into tears. We all stared at him. He pushed his steel helmet well over his face, but we could see the tears pouring down over his thin cheeks. He looked not a day more than seventeen. None of the other men said a word to him. Indeed, they all looked exhausted and fed-up enough to cry.

The older soldier pushed his helmet high and wiped the sweat off his forehead. 'They've been telling us that tale about General Wenk for weeks. What do they take us for? General Wenk won't come. God alone knows where he is. The Russians are everywhere. They're just playing cat and mouse with us. And so we go on . . . fighting to the last man.' His voice rose in mockery of Hitler's speeches. 'Fighting to the last little boy, they ought to say.' He turned and looked at the weeping soldier. The awful bitterness in the soldier's voice, still urging his little group on to some kind of action, brought tears to my eyes.

From E. Wendel, *Hausfrau at War*, Odhams Press, 1957.

Questions

1 Who was doing the 'terror bombing' of Germany?

2 In what ways did Hitler use the fear of the Russians to build resistance?

3 How might this order be used to show that Germany was almost defeated?

4 What can you learn from Else Wendel's account (B) about the condition of the German armies in Berlin?

5 How successful was the older soldier likely to be in urging his men to action?

6 From these two extracts build up your own account of what it must have been like in Germany in April 1945.

39 Berlin: death and glory

As the Allies closed in on Berlin Hitler remained in his headquarters' bunker there. On 28 April 1945 he married Eva Braun and then, just after midnight on the following day, they committed suicide. Goebbels and his wife Magda committed suicide on 1 May after Magda had poisoned their children. Source A is from The Berlin Bunker *by James P. O'Donnell, 1979. The book is based on O'Donnell's research and interviews with survivors.*

Just about the time that Hitler and Eva Braun killed themselves the Russians raised a banner over the Reichstag – the parliament building in Berlin. Extract B is taken from The Road to Berlin *(1983) by the historian John Erickson, who is an expert on Soviet military affairs. The photograph (C) was taken by Khaldei, a correspondent for the Soviet newspaper* Pravda *and was titled 'Victory'.*

A Death in the bunker

General Mohnke gives us a last, crisp, eyewitness account of the living Goebbels. 'Going over to the coat-rack in the small room that had served as his study, he donned his hat, his scarf, his long uniform overcoat. Slowly, he drew on his kid gloves, making each finger snug. Then, like a cavalier, he offered his right arm to his wife. They were wordless now. So were we three spectators. Slowly but steadily, leaning a bit on each other, they headed up the stairs to the courtyard.'

For both Joseph and Magda Goebbels had carefully rehearsed Professor Haase's approved Bunker method, pistol and poison. Magda went first. She bit into her capsule, sank slowly to the soft spring earth. She was wearing, for a brooch, Adolf Hitler's golden party badge, which the Führer had given her as a parting present the day before his own death. Her husband fired a bullet into the back of her blonde head. Goebbels then bit into his own capsule, squeezed the trigger of his Walther P-38 pistol, and put a bullet through his right temple. The FBK officer called for Captain Schwaegermann and together they performed a hasty cremation. The cans of petrol were poured over the bodies and then set alight. 'There are two ways in this world to judge a man,' Hitler had said as long ago as 1927, 'the kind of woman he marries, and the way he dies.' Unwittingly, Hitler had uttered a fitting epitaph not only for himself but for his own prophet, Goebbels.

From J. P. O'Donnell, The Berlin Bunker, Dent, 1979.

B Glory over the Reichstag

'Gde Znamiya?' – 'Where is the Banner?': Colonel Zinchenko's repeated question was answered with the report that it was in good hands, everyone in the battalion knew Yegorov and Kantariya and that the Banner was well on the way to being raised over the Reichstag. In the thick and murky atmosphere of the entrance hall to the Reichstag Zinchenko summoned Yegorov and Kantariya, talked briefly with them and then addressed them in very homely terms: 'Well then,

From J. Erickson, The Road to Berlin, Weidenfeld and Nicolson, 1983.

off you go, lads and stick the Banner up there'. At 1800 hours on the evening of 30 April a second assault went in, bursting through the machine-gunners in the upper levels and succeeding at 2250 hours in planting the Victory Banner high over the Reichstag, though it was many hours before the entire building was cleared.

C 'Victory'

The Russian flag is waved in victory over the Reichstag in Berlin, 1 May 1945.

Questions

1 Suggest reasons why Hitler and Goebbels committed suicide.

2 Why were the bodies burnt?

3 Historians have spent a lot of time and effort in finding out exactly what happened in the last days in the Berlin bunker. Why have they done so?

4 What does this photograph and the one on the flag raising on Iwo Jima (page 3) suggest about the importance of flags in battle?

5 Why did the Russian colonel want the flag raised even before the building was cleared of Germans?

40 Kamikaze

The Japanese were determined to halt the American advance in the Pacific. Kamikaze planes were turned into flying bombs and Japanese pilots willingly volunteered to fly these planes into targets. The letter is from one such pilot, Akio Otsuka. It was published in 1956 in a book called The Sun Goes Down *by Jean Lantigung. Kamikaze means 'divine wind', named after a typhoon which saved Japan from Mongol invasion in the thirteenth century. The photograph shows American forces massed at Okinawa in April 1945.*

A Preparing for suicide

Contrary to my usual habit, I woke early, at five o'clock. I did my exercises stripped to the waist. I felt extremely well.

Now one has only to place a sheet of paper into the little box which usually contains the ashes of the dead. I wonder if that is true? I wanted to send you parings of my nails and a few locks of my hair, but I had my hair cut yesterday and my nails are already too short. I am sorry, but unfortunately it is too late. Neither my nails nor my hair will grow again in one night.

I do not want a grave. I would feel oppressed if they were to put me into a narrow vault. A vagabond, such as I, has no need of it. Will you tell my parents that?

Do not weep because I am about to die. If I were to live and one of my dear ones to die, I would do all in my power to cheer those who remain behind. I would try to be brave.

11.30 a.m. – the last morning. I shall now have breakfast and then go to the aerodrome. I am busy with my final briefing and have no time to write any more. So I bid you farewell.

Excuse this illegible letter and the jerky sentences.

Keep in good health.

I believe in the victory of Greater Asia.

I pray for the happiness of you all, and I beg your forgiveness for my lack of piety.

I leave for the attack with a smile on my face. The moon will be full to-night. As I fly over the open sea off Okinawa I will choose the enemy ship that is to be my target.

I will show you that I know how to die bravely.

With all my respectful affection.

From Jean Lantigung (ed.), *The Sun Goes Down*, William Kimber, 1956.

B Target for destruction

Questions

1 What does the letter tell us about the mind of a Kamikaze pilot?

2 What does the pilot mean by 'the victory of Greater Asia'?

3 Why should Akio Otsuka have wished to send nail parings and locks of his hair home to Japan?

4 Is there any similarity between Hitler's last order (page 76) and the Japanese use of Kamikaze planes?

5 Does the picture show the military reason for such suicide attacks?

41 The atomic bomb

As early as August 1939 President Roosevelt had received a letter from Albert Einstein, a Jewish scientist who had fled from Germany, saying that a nuclear chain reaction could provide a powerful new bomb. The first extract is from Einstein's letter.

The Americans set up the Manhattan Project and by the summer of 1945 they had developed three atomic bombs. One was used as a test; the second was dropped on Hiroshima, 6 August 1945; the third was used against Nagasaki, 9 August 1945. The Japanese surrendered unconditionally five days later. Source B is taken from the account of a visit made to Hiroshima by Marcel Junod, shortly after the Japanese surrender.

A Einstein's warning

In the course of the last four months it has been made probable – through the work of Joliot in France as well as Fermi and Sziliard in America – that it may become possible to set up a nuclear chain reaction in a large mass of uranium, by which vast amounts of power and large quantities of new radium-like elements would be generated. Now it appears almost certain that this could be achieved in the immediate future.

This new phenomenon would also lead to the construction of bombs, and it is conceivable – though much less certain – that extremely powerful bombs of a new type may thus be constructed. A single bomb of this type, carried by boat and exploded in a port, might very well destroy the whole port together with some of the surrounding territory. However, such bombs might very well prove to be too heavy for transportation by air.

From Tony Howarth, *Twentieth Century History*, Longman, 1979.

B Hiroshima, August 1945

At three-quarters of a mile [1.2 kilometres] from the centre of the explosion nothing at all was left. Everything had disappeared. It was a stony waste littered with debris and twisted girders. The incandescent breath of the fire has swept away every obstacle and all that remained upright were one or two fragments of stone walls and a few stoves which had remained incongruously on their base.

We got out of the car and made our way slowly through the ruins into the centre of the dead city. Absolute silence reigned in the whole necropolis. There was not even a survivor searching in the ruins, though some distance away a group of soldiers were clearing a passage through the debris. Here and there a little grass was beginning to sprout amidst the ruins, but there was not a bird or an animal to be seen anywhere.

. . . A young Japanese doctor accompanied me to the train when I left to return to Tokyo.

On what remained of the station facade the hands of the clock had been stopped by the fire at 8.15.

It was perhaps the first time in the history of humanity that the birth of a new era was recorded on the face of a clock.

From Marcel Junod, *Warrier Without Weapons*, Jonathan Cape, 1961.

Questions

1 What detail of Einstein's statement was proved wrong by the Manhattan Project?

2 Fewer people died at Hiroshima than Dresden. Does Marcel Junod's account suggest why Hiroshima was thought to be the more terrible raid?

3 In what way did this event mark the birth of a new era?

4 What consequences of atomic weapons are not mentioned in either source?

Part 8

Costs and consequences

42 The cost of victory

Victory in 1945 was won only at an enormous cost in human lives and suffering. Source A shows the estimated total of deaths by soldiers and civilians from six years of war. Source B was taken by Yergeni Khaldci, one of the Soviet official war correspondents. It was given the title 'Home to Ruin' and was taken in 1942. Source C is from a message left by Vice-Admiral Onishi, commandant of the Kamikaze pilots, to the Japanese people.

A The cost of war

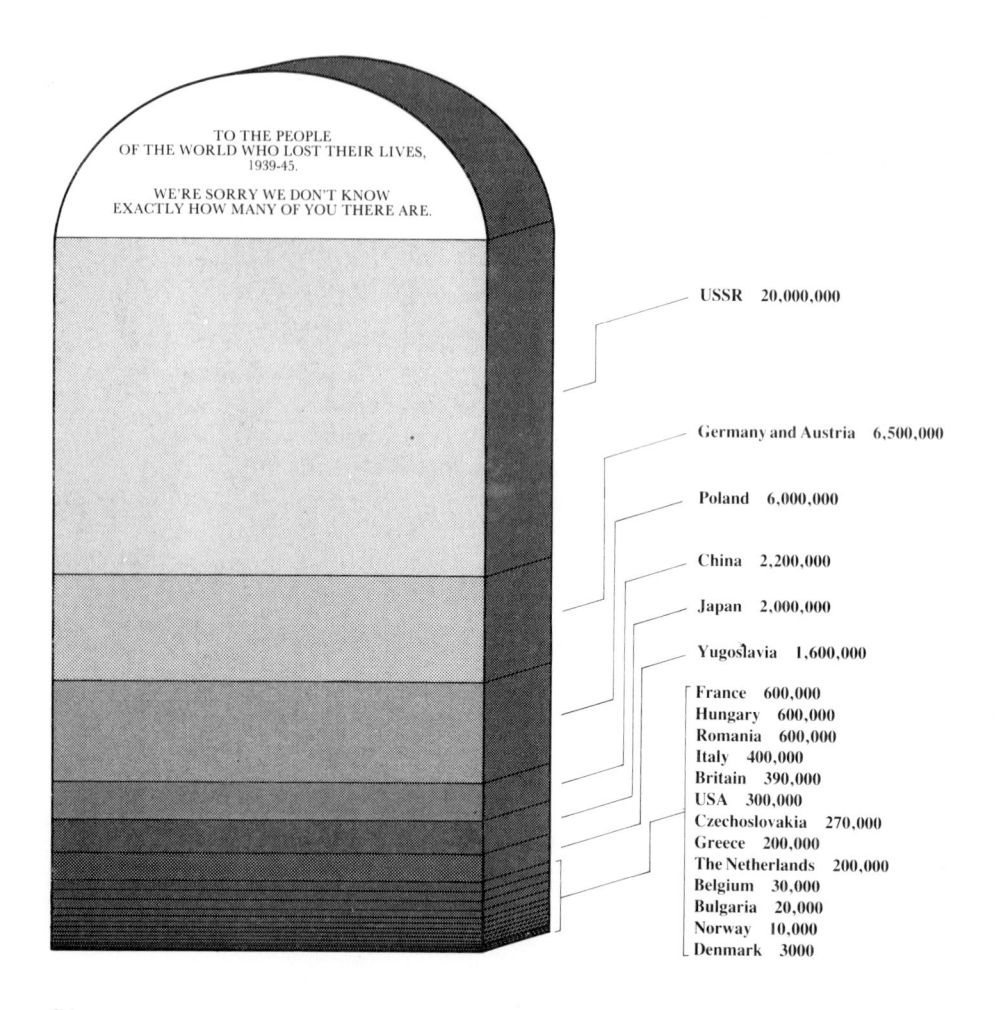

TO THE PEOPLE
OF THE WORLD WHO LOST THEIR LIVES,
1939-45.

WE'RE SORRY WE DON'T KNOW
EXACTLY HOW MANY OF YOU THERE ARE.

USSR 20,000,000
Germany and Austria 6,500,000
Poland 6,000,000
China 2,200,000
Japan 2,000,000
Yugoslavia 1,600,000
France 600,000
Hungary 600,000
Romania 600,000
Italy 400,000
Britain 390,000
USA 300,000
Czechoslovakia 270,000
Greece 200,000
The Netherlands 200,000
Belgium 30,000
Bulgaria 20,000
Norway 10,000
Denmark 3000

B 'Home to Ruin'

C The Kamikaze spirit

'I speak to the spirits of the Kamikaze boys. You have fought well. You have my abiding gratitude. You have died as Human Bullets, convinced of final victory which did not come true. I wish my death to express my regret and sorrow to you and to your loved ones left behind.

'To you young men living now in Japan:

'I shall be happy in the Beyond if my death will show you that any reckless action will only worry the Emperor. You must carry out His Majesty's wish. Bear the unbearable and do not lose pride in being Japanese. You are the treasures of Japan. Hold tight the Kamikaze spirit and use it for the welfare of Japan and the peace of the world.'

From Gwen Terusaki, *Bridge to the Sun*, Michael Joseph, 1958.

Questions

1 Which part of the world was the biggest killing ground?

2 The USSR, Yugoslavia and Poland each lost 10 per cent of the population. What effects would this have a) on ordinary families; and b) on government fear for the future?

3 How does the picture (B) catch the feeling of the heavy cost of the war for the Russians?

4 What was the 'unbearable' to the Japanese soldiers?

5 How could the destructive force of Kamikaze be used for the welfare of Japan?

43 Home fronts 1945

The war had involved everybody and women at home had to bear a very great strain as they carried on the routine of life from day to day. Source A is taken from Nella Last's War, *1981. Nella Last kept a diary from September 1939 as part of a detailed record of her life made for a mass-observation project. Source B is from Ruth Evans' translation of her German mother's diary which she made for her children during the war years in Hamburg. Mathilde Wolff-Mönckeberg, Ruth's mother, survived the war, and the diary lay forgotten in an old Italian settle for many years. In 1979 Ruth Evans translated and edited the diary which was then published as a book,* On the Other Side *by Mathilde Wolff-Mönckeberg. The photograph is of Berlin in June 1945 and was taken by a Soviet photographer.*

A Britain

Saturday 14 July 1945.
A violent thunderstorm raged in the night, and at 2.30 I rose and took two aspirins. I felt I could have flown with nerves. I don't like taking them; they make me drowsy when I need to get up, and this morning I had to go downtown for a hair appointment. Queues were everywhere, for wedge-heeled shoes, pork-pies, fish, bread and cakes, tomatoes – and emergency ration-cards at the food office. I stared at one fish shop – all the marble slab was covered and fringed with bracken, and the fish set out attractively. Granted it did not smell fresh enough for me (I'm fussy about stale-smelling food) but I felt as if the war was over! There was some chocolate too, in one window – and quite an assortment of sweets. I caught snatches of conversation about the discussion in the papers on queues. I looked searchingly down the queues for any signs of 'nervy women on the verge of breakdown' but they looked pretty robust, if a bit impatient.

From N. Last, *Nella Last's War*, Falling Wall Press, 1981.

B Germany

6 July 1945
Tired, tired. If anything this summer is even more difficult than the last. We are very short of food and one's entire interest is concentrated in this direction. It is the absence of fat which makes one so greedy. I have fantastic visions of sausages, beefsteaks, luscious cakes with whipped cream, large bowls of fruit, platters of mixed vegetables – young peas, beans, red tomatoes, pale green cucumbers, tender cauliflower and provocative asparagus with butter, a dance of inviting and alluring things before my mind's eye. At the best delicatessen shop in town you get a bit of mince and dehydrated vegetables that taste like straw, no potatoes, and at best an indefinable brew of soup. If only one could exist without food! I am going to bed, it is cold and grey, not a pleasant summer evening. Irmgard Lieven, Gisela Markert's sister, and her eight-month-old baby are staying with us.

From M. Wolff-Mönckeberg, *On the Other Side*, Peter Owen, 1979.

C In the ruins of Berlin, 1945

Questions

1 What do both accounts have in common?

2 List the differences which you can find in the two accounts.

3 Can you find evidence in Source B that it is written by somebody living in a defeated country?

4 Does the photograph show the nature of the problem faced by civilians in both Britain and Germany?

5 What evidence is there that the photograph is taken in a German city in 1945?

44 Potsdam and a divided Germany

At the last wartime conference, held at Potsdam from 17 July to 2 August 1945, Stalin, Attlee (newly elected prime minister of Britain) and Truman (president of the United States following Roosevelt's death) set down the terms for a defeated Germany while the war against Japan continued. The map shows the way in which the occupation of Germany was arranged and the extract is taken from the Potsdam declaration.

A   Germany and Poland 1945

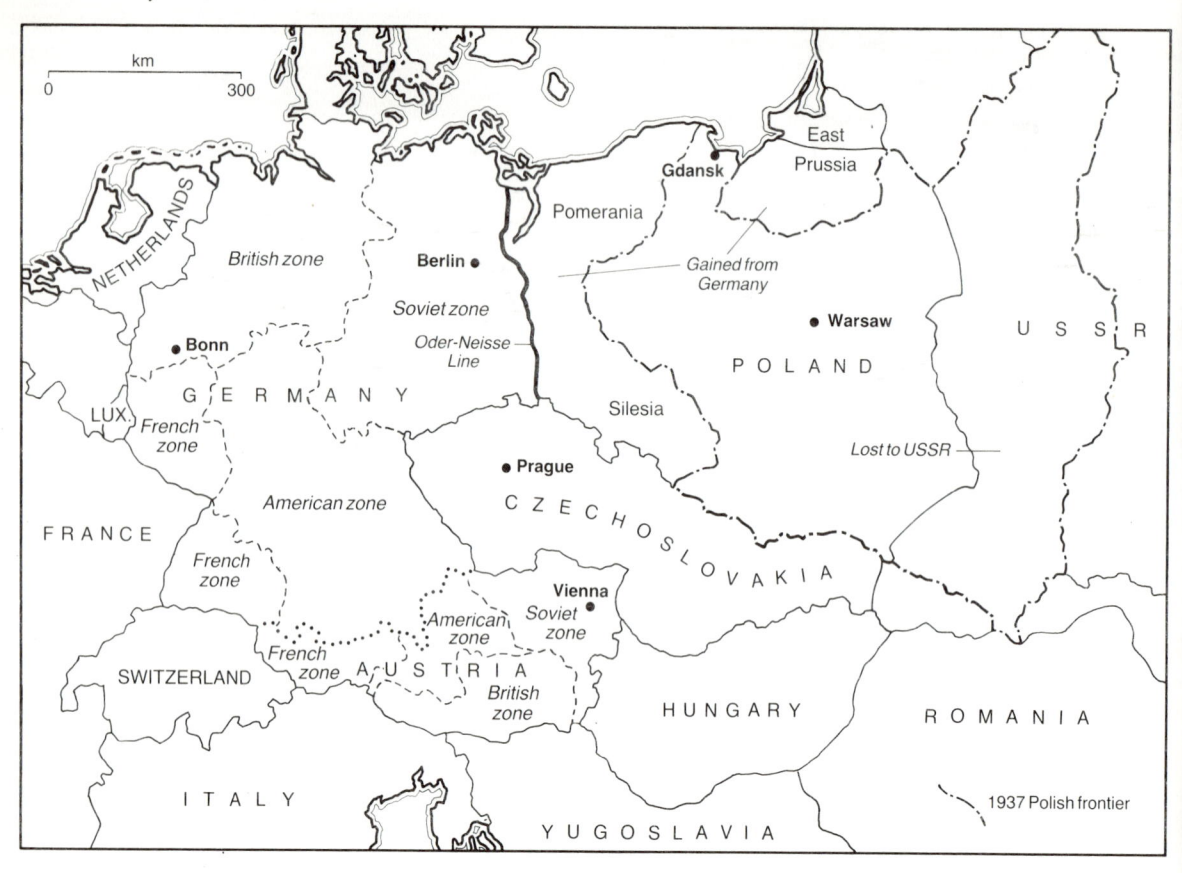

B The Potsdam declaration

The Allied armies are in occupation of the whole of Germany and the German people have begun to atone for the terrible crimes committed under the leadership of those whom in the hour of their success, they openly approved and blindly obeyed.

... It is not the intention of the Allies to destroy or enslave the German people: It is the intention of the Allies that the German people be given the opportunity to prepare for the eventual reconstruction of their life on a democratic and peaceful basis. If their own efforts are steadily directed to this end, it will be possible for them in due course to take their place among the free and peaceful peoples of the world.

From L. L. Snyder, *Fifty Major Documents of the Twentieth Century*, Anvil Books, Van Nostrand, 1955.

Questions

1 Look carefully at the map and work out possible consequences of the special position of Berlin.

2 Compare this map with the map on page 6. What different boundary between Poland and Germany can you see?

3 What affect have the occupation arrangements had on the post-war history of Germany and Europe?

4 In what ways were the German people atoning for the crimes of their leaders?

5 Why would some people have objected to the Germans being given the chance to reconstruct their national life? What sort of arguments would they have used?

45 Nuremburg

The public trial of twenty-two Nazi leaders began at Nuremburg in November 1945. They were tried for crimes against peace, against humanity and against defenceless minorities. Eleven were sentenced to death by hanging. Source A is from the trial judgement on Goering. The picture was painted in 1946 by Dame Laura Knight who was sent as an official artist to the trials. She was determined to remain objective and concentrated on the problems of painting the courtroom scene. She had to travel back and forth from her hotel to the court and the devastation of the city. In her final painting the blank wall of the courtroom contained a vision of the ruined city. She said to the committee that had sent her to Nuremburg, 'In that ruined city death and destruction are ever present. They had to come into the picture'.

A The trial of Goering

Goering: From the moment he joined the party in 1922 and took command of the street fighting organization, the SA, Goering was the adviser, the active agent of Hitler and one of the prime leaders of the Nazi movement. As Hitler's political deputy he was largely instrumental in bringing the National Socialists to power in 1933, and was charged with consolidating this power and expanding the German armed might. He developed the Gestapo and created the first concentration camps, relinquishing them to Himmler in 1934. . . .

Goering commanded the Luftwaffe in the attack on Poland and throughout the aggressive wars which followed. . . . The record is filled with Goering's admissions of his complicity in the use of slave labour. . . .

Goering persecuted the Jews, particularly after the November 1938 riots, and not only in Germany, where he raised the billion mark fine as stated elsewhere, but in the conquered territories as well. . . . There is nothing to be said in mitigation. . . . His guilt is unique in its enormity. The record discloses no excuse for this man.

VERDICT: GUILTY on all four counts.
SENTENCE: Death by hanging.

From L. L. Snyder, *Fifty Major Documents of the Twentieth Century*, Anvil Books, Van Nostrand, 1955.

B The Nuremburg courtroom

Questions

1 From your reading of the verdict suggest what four counts Goering might have been charged with.

2 Did the record of Goering's crimes justify the sentence?

3 Why do you think Laura Knight painted the picture as she did?

4 In what ways does this painting add to your understanding of the Nuremburg trials?

5 How would you define a war criminal?

46 Refugees and repatriation

After the war there were millions of displaced people. Germans were expelled from Poland, Czechoslovakia and other east European countries. Others fled from the Soviet zone in east Germany. There were Jews and other people freed from German labour camps, often with no home or relatives. Photograph A appeared in Picture Post *in 1947 and gives a human face to the massive refugee problem.*

Many minority people in the USSR so hated the Communists that they had fought alongside the Germans. Among them were Cossacks from south Russia who in earlier times had been the most loyal soldiers (or 'royal officers') in the Tsar's armies. Many were captured by the British in 1944 and 1945. At the wartime Conference at Yalta in 1945 the British agreed to return these prisoners of war to the Soviet Union, although the Communist government would take revenge on them for being 'counter-revolutionaries'. One Cossack who was forced to return against his will was Nikolai Krasnov who later got to freedom in Sweden after surviving Soviet labour camps. Source B describes how he and his father were questioned in the Lubianka prison in Moscow, which was run by the secret police (then the MGB). The prison chief was Merkulov and he mentions one of the Cossack leaders or Atamans who had sent an appeal for help to the west. He also refers to the river Oder in Germany. The extract was quoted in Victims of Yalta *(1977) by Nikolai Tolstoy, who was born in England but whose father was a count from White Russia who had fled after the Communists seized power in 1917. Before Nikolai Tolstoy's book, the story of how the British had handed their prisoners over to the USSR had been known by only a few people.*

A Refugees

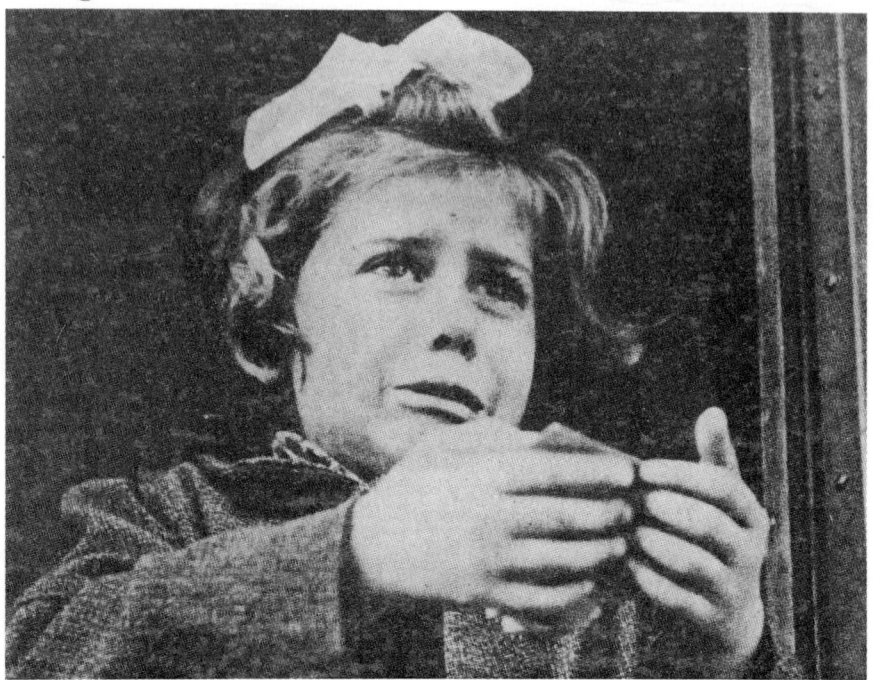

A child refugee in Europe, 1947.

B Soviet prisoners in the Lubianka prison

Merkulov paused, and then switched his attack to young Nikolai. 'What kind of muscles do you have, king's officer? I'll send you to a place where you'll sing a different tune! You will make good what those Fascist swine ruined. It's too bad that we hauled in so few of you young counter-revolutionaries. Too many of you got off the hook and are hiding under the petticoats of the West. Never mind. We'll get them later on. We'll dredge them up from the bottom of the sea!

'You will not get a bullet in your forehead. Not in your forehead and not in the back of your head. We will make you live. Live and work! The time will come when your life will be given for the sake of socialist construction.'

'I think this conversation is not leading anywhere,' my father broke in sharply. 'Whaaat?' roared the General of the MGB. 'Do you realise where you are and with whom you are speaking? In Lubianka! With Merkulov! I am boss here. I say what I please. Did you get anything out of your petition that your dear Ataman drew up in French and sent from Spittal? Do you think we didn't know about that? No one will help you, not your Churchills or your Trumans, not kings or diplomats. When we roar they sit tight on their tails! I am told that there were Tsars who watered their horses in the Oder. Well, the time will come when we will water Soviet horses in the Thames!'

After this outburst, Merkulov pressed a bell and dismissed the two Krasnovs, father and son.

From Nikolai Tolstoy, *Victims of Yalta*, Hodder and Stoughton, 1977.

Questions

1 How far does one photograph depict the tragedy of all the homeless and displaced?

2 Why do you think there were so many refugees in Europe after the war?

3 What does Merkulov say will happen to the Krasnovs?

4 Suggest some examples of what the 'Fascist swine ruined'.

5 How many clues can you find to show that the wartime alliance of the USSR and Western powers had begun to break down?

47 Writers and the war

As with the First World War, the Second World War strongly influenced novelists and poets of the time. Joseph Heller, an American novelist, wrote his novel Catch-22 *(Source A) to show the stupidity that goes with war. 'Catch-22' has become part of the language with its message that to avoid something you have to accept something worse. Heller's novel was published in the United States in 1955. A pilot, Yossarian, is discussing another pilot, Orr, with the air force doctor, Daneeka. Orr was suffering from the effects of flying too many dangerous combat missions but wouldn't give up.*

Adrian Henri, poet, painter and singer, was born at Birkenhead in 1932. Source B is taken from his poem Autobiography *and comes from Part One (1932–51)*

A Catch-22

Yossarian looked at him soberly and tried another approach. 'Is Orr crazy?'

'He sure is,' Doc Daneeka said.

'Can you ground him?'

'I sure can. But first he has to ask me to. That's part of the rule.'

'Then why doesn't he ask you to?'

'Because he's crazy,' Doc Daneeka said. 'He has to be crazy to keep flying combat missions after all the close calls he's had. Sure, I can ground Orr. But first he has to ask me to.'

'That's all he has to do to be grounded?'

'That's all. Let him ask me.'

'And then you can ground him?' Yossarian asked.

'No. Then I can't ground him.'

'You mean there's a catch?'

'Sure there's a catch,' Doc Daneeka replied. 'Catch-22. Anyone who wants to get out of combat duty isn't really crazy.'

There was only one catch and that was Catch-22, which specified that a concern for one's own safety in the face of dangers that were real and immediate was the process of a rational mind. Orr was crazy and could be grounded. All he had to to was ask, and as soon as he did, he would no longer be crazy and would have to fly more missions. Orr would be crazy to fly more missions and sane if he didn't, but if he was sane he had to fly them. If he flew them he was crazy and didn't have to, but if he didn't want to he was sane and had to. Yossarian was moved very deeply by the absolute simplicity of this clause of Catch-22 and let out a respectful whistle.

'That's some catch, that Catch-22,' he observed.

'It's the best there is,' Doc Daneeka agreed.

From Joseph Heller, *Catch-22*, Jonathan Cape, 1962.

B Memories

carrying my gasmask to school every day
buying savings stamps
remembering my National Registration Number
(ZMGM/136/3 see I can still remember it)
avoiding Careless Talk Digging for Victory
looking for German spies everywhere
Oh yes, I did my bit for my country that long dark winter,
me and Winston and one or two others,
wearing my tin hat whenever possible
singing 'Hang out the Washing on the Siegfried Line'
aircraft-recognition charts pinned to my bedroom wall
the smell of paint on toy soldiers
doing paintings of Spitfires and Hurricanes, Lancasters and Halifaxes
always with a Heinkel or a Messerschmitt plunging helplessly
   into the sea in the background
pink light in the sky from Liverpool burning 150 miles away
the thunder of daylight flying fortresses high overhead shaking the
   elderberry-tree
bright barrage balloons flying over the docks
morning curve of the bay seen from the park on the hill
after coming out of the air raid shelter
listening for the 'All Clear' siren
listening to Vera Lynn Dorothy Lamour Allen Jones and
   The Andrew Sisters
clutching my father's hand tripping over the unfamiliar kerb
I walk over every day
in the blackout

From Adrian Henri, Roger McGough, Brian Patten: New Volume, Penguin, 1983.

Questions

1 In your own words explain how 'Catch-22' worked in the case described in Source A.

2 What does it suggest about Joseph Heller's view of the effects of war?

3 What evidence is there that Adrian Henri is giving a young boy's memory of wartime?

4 How many references to government efforts to involve civilians in the struggle for victory can you find?

5 In what ways would a German schoolboy's memories be different from those of Adrian Henri?

Further reading

Fifteen books, mainly novels, about the Second World War that are readily available:

J. G. Ballard, *Empire of the Sun*, Granada, 1985 (war in the Far East).
Christabel Bielenberg, *The Past is Myself*, Corgi, 1984 (life in Nazi Germany).
Len Deighton, *Bomber*, Panther, 1978 (British bomber raids).
Nicholas Gage, *Eleni*, Fontana, 1984 (war in Greece).
Graham Greene, *The End of the Affair*, Penguin, 1970 (home front).
Joseph Heller, *Catch-22*, Corgi, 1969 (American bomber force).
David Hughes, *The Pork Butcher*, Penguin, 1985 (German occupation of France).
Masuji Ibuse, *Black Ruin*, Bantam Books, 1985 (the atomic bomb).
Thomas Keneally, *Schindler's Ark*, Coronet Books, 1983 (the death camps).
W. S. Kuniczak, *Valedictory*, Sphere, 1985 (Polish war effort).
Nicholas Monsarrat, *The Cruel Sea*, Penguin, 1983 (war at sea).
Eric Newby, *Love and War in the Apennines*, Pan Books, 1983 (Italian campaign).
Irwin Shaw, *The Young Lions*, New English Library, 1985 (Americans in Europe).
A. J. P. Taylor, *The Russian War, 1941–45*, Jonathan Cape, 1978 (collection of Soviet photographs).
Evelyn Waugh, *Sword of Honour Trilogy*, Penguin, 1970 (British in the Middle East).